Vanishing Americana

NEW YORK: A. S. BARNES AND COMPANY, INC.
LONDON: THOMAS YOSELOFF, LTD.

VANISHING AMERICANA

BY EVERETT B. WILSON

A. S. Barnes and Company, Inc.
11 East 36th Street
New York 16, N. Y.

Thomas Yoseloff, Ltd.
123 New Bond Street
London W.1, England

Printed in the United States of America

First printing January 1961

Second printing April 1963

Dedication

This book is dedicated to my grandchildren and to Johnny McDonald, Christina and Jaquelyn Larson, Nancy May Hoberman, and the several other fine American youngsters whose photographs appear in its pages. Had they been born a few years later, they would have missed many of the Americana shown herein. Some already are impossible to find except in museums.

Picture Credits

Most of the photographs appearing in this book were made by the author. For those pictures provided by other sources—Baltimore and Ohio Railroad, Great Northern Railway, Library of Congress, Norfolk and Western Railway—the author hereby makes known his gratitude.

Contents

Vanishing Americana

Introduction:
Our Changing American Life

The United States is noted for rapid and sweeping changes in its ideas, its customs, and its way of life. Some of these changes are for the better, and some are not.

This volume represents an attempt to report on and picture the more significant and interesting changes which either are taking place or have already occurred.

Things change fast in this country, so what is deemed essential and can be seen on all sides today may be almost impossible to find tomorrow. The speed with which the spread of rural electric power led to the virtual disappearance of the working windmill is an example.

Many Americana, like the windmill, have vanished from all but a handful of places. Some will remain for a long while because their owners cherish them as reminders of the past.

No effort has been made to report on changes in either male or female attire, except for a few understandable cases. Both subjects are too unpredictable and complex to discuss here. There also has been no attempt to describe the vast changes which have taken place in our industrial and commercial processes, except where they touch the public directly.

Inevitably, there will be differences of opinion as to what has vanished and what hasn't, as to what is in the process of vanishing and what isn't, but those are matters of judgment. Doubtless many omissions will be suggested; however, the question of relative importance must be considered.

1. Our Changing Farms

Electricity and gasoline have been responsible for many vital changes and for many improvements on American farms, including running water, refrigeration, and motive power.

The automobile and truck have brought the farmer many minutes, and sometimes many hours, closer to town and market, with the result that he now can buy conveniently all of the food items that he formerly had to produce on the farm. In many cases, the foods he buys are of better quality, more sanitary, and actually cost him less, considering his time, than those he used to produce himself.

That is why livestock and poultry and the farm garden and orchard are disappearing from farms on which they are not used in commercial production.

Moreover, the farmer no longer needs to be self-sufficient in other respects. He now can buy from a store or mail-order house all of the articles he formerly had to make on the farm or go without. Thus, it is only natural that the devices once used in making cloth, butter, lard, and other items are disappearing rapidly.

Because he can buy the things he needs, the farmer is becoming a specialist, devoting his time, energy, and capital, not to mention his land, to those carefully selected commercial crops that will yield him the best return. Thanks to all the new time- and labor-saving devices and the elimination of livestock which once took up so much of his time, the farmer and his family are leading a more pleasant and less isolated life. The farmer with no cows to milk and no horses to feed, curry, and harness often sleeps later in the morning and hence can stay up later at night.

He accomplishes more with less physical effort and, thanks to television and radio, he is as well informed as his city cousin. The disappearance of the Americana which once were the very backbone of the farm may seem regrettable to many, but for the most part the farmer and his family are living better without them, and that is what really counts.

A century-old barn.

The Farm Buildings

Every farm had and still has at least one barn, sometimes several of them. There was the large, main barn where the horses were kept and the cows were housed and milked, with a loft overhead containing hay and straw. The loft was a favorite place for farm youngsters to play on rainy days or when they wanted to be alone with special friends. Adults also used the hayloft occasionally as an overflow place to sleep or for other more interesting purposes.

If there are no cows or horses left on the farm, the old barn may have been allowed to become so decrepit as to be on the point of collapse from old age.

In addition to the barn and pump house, and of course the farm home, there also were numerous other buildings on larger farms. For example, you always found a privy and might also have found some or all of the following: milk house, smokehouse, woodshed, stable, carriage shed, chicken coop, hog house or pigpen, wash house, spring house, icehouse, root or vegetable cellar, corn crib, storm cellar, and others.

Today, the typical farmer needs little more than a building that serves as a garage and tool or implement shed, plus maybe a cow barn, corn crib, and chicken house, but even those are becoming scarce. The other older buildings, if still standing, usually are serving as storage places or else just falling down.

The spring house.

The Spring House

If the farm was blessed with a good flowing spring, you often found a spring house built over it. Here, the frugal farmer placed cans of milk, tubs of butter, and other perishables which benefited from the low temperature of running water.

The flow of the spring tended to make the inside of the spring house relatively cool in hot weather and thus made it suitable for the storage of other foods that needed protection from summer heat. It was also the coolest place on the farm to sit and rest on torrid days.

The icehouse.

The Icehouse

When the northern farmer had a nearby lake or pond, he usually had an icehouse where he stored the precious ice harvested after the first good freeze. To slow up melting, the icehouse was built on the side of a hill, under the shade of a large tree, and the ice was covered with sawdust. Cakes of ice were carried in as needed to the icebox, located in the kitchen or on the back porch of the farm home.

Mechanical refrigeration and the freezer have demoted the icehouse, if indeed it still stands, to a mere storage place.

The Smokehouse.

The Smokehouse

The small building where carcasses of pork were cut up and smoked was called the smokehouse. It was an active place at butchering time, usually in early winter when the outside temperature was low.

The smokehouse sometimes could be recognized by a chimney but often there was none, because it was desirable to keep the smoke from escaping. As a result, you can still smell the hickory smoke in an old smokehouse that has not been used as such for many years.

The farmer who still raises meat animals for his own use, and the number is growing steadily smaller, doesn't need a smokehouse or butchering shed these days. He either sends his animals to the locker plant to be slaughtered or else has the work done by an itinerant butcher. He freezes the meat he doesn't consume fresh and buys his smoked meat at the supermarket; so the smokehouse, too, is becoming a novelty on the modern farm.

A slave house.

The Slave House

Before slavery was abolished, farms in southern and border states had slave quarters in which their slaves lived. Some of them were rather miserable buildings.

Any slave house standing today is being used for other purposes, such as storing feed or fertilizer or other farm supplies.

The slave house has been replaced on larger farms by tenant houses and farm workers' homes, many of which have all the basic conveniences of the farmer's own home.

The Stable.

The Stable

On some farms, there is one building still in use that hasn't changed much in appearance through the years, although its use has changed radically. That building is the stable, formerly the place where the farmer kept his horses and their harness.

Each horse had a stall, so he wouldn't kick his stablemates. Young boys on farms spent many an hour carrying hay, straw, corn, and other feed to the stalls and cleaning them.

The stable often had space for storing a carriage or two or a buggy, although those vehicles sometimes were kept in a separate building known as a carriage shed, just as the horses sometimes were kept in a barn with the cows.

These same stables and carriage sheds are being used today to house the successors to the farm horse—the truck and tractor and automobile—with or without alterations.

Harness room.

The Harness Room

The harness used on farm horses was kept either in a separate room or on pegs in the stable or barn near the horse's stall. There you found the bridles and bits, blinders, reins, checkreins, collars, girths, cruppers, breeching, traces, and blankets.

With the passing of the horse from the farm, the harness either has been sold or discarded or else hangs collecting dust on the same old pegs, a silent reminder of the day when the horse was king.

Work horses.

The Work Horse

Not so many years ago, the work horse was the backbone of the American farm. But today he has been replaced almost entirely by the truck and tractor. The number of farmers still relying on the horse, or the mule, to do their hauling and cultivating grows steadily smaller.

Most farms had at least one pair, or team, of sturdy work horses which were used to cultivate the land and haul crops to market, and also to pull carriages and buggies if there were no light-harness horses on the place. Horses were as common as cows and pigs in those days and much more useful.

Of the few work horses remaining on farms today, most get hitched up only occasionally, so that most farm boys no longer need to know how to harness and curry horses or how to drive a stubborn mule.

A close-up.

A well-matched team.

Jennie, the mule, and friend.

A stallion.

Mare and foal.

A human yoke.

The horse collar.

An ox yoke.

The Horse Collar

This strange object is disappearing even faster than the horse, because riding and hunting horses don't use it. It's a horse collar, part of the harness put on the farm horse when he was being used to pull a wagon or plow.

The leather collar went around the horse's neck and was heavily padded to ease the discomfort of pulling heavy loads.

In addition, two related objects known as yokes were found on early farms. One kind was placed on the necks of oxen when harnessing them to a cart or plow. Another kind was used by humans to ease the task of carrying two heavy pails of water from a distant pump or well. Both were made of wood.

Currying a horse.

The Curry Comb

Another chore for the busy farm boy was currying the horses to remove filth and dirt and improve their general appearance. The job was accomplished with a metal curry comb, found today only where saddle horses are kept.

Shoeing the Horses

Farm horses had to have their shoes replaced regularly, and there is a job that takes real skill. Some farmers learned to do the job themselves; others had it done in town by a blacksmith or else retained the services of a traveling horseshoer who came to the farm.

Shoeing a horse involved removing the old worn shoe, cleaning and paring the hoof, heating and beating the new iron shoe into the right shape, and then nailing it into place. Often a dressing was added to make the hoof look a little neater. If the horse was at all nervous or unruly, considerable brute strength as well as agility were required on the part of the horseshoer.

Here is one more hard job that has disappeared from the farm. Even those farmers who now keep saddle horses rarely do their own shoeing.

Shoeing a horse.

The horsewhip.

The Horsewhip

A long, slender whip with a lash on the end was deemed indispensable by all who drove horses on the farm or elsewhere. The whip—made of rattan or whalebone or a holly or hickory branch, often with a leather covering—served to keep the horses moving when they showed a tendency to slow down and to stimulate an extra burst of speed when the driver was in a hurry.

The horsewhip also served as a weapon with which to chastise anyone who might anger the owner, such as a trespasser or poacher or an unwelcome suitor.

Merely making a cracking sound by snapping the lash over the horse's head or gently flicking his rear often was all that was needed to get the desired response, but sometimes the whip was applied vigorously to get a sure reaction. Needless to say, the whip has become as scarce on the farm as the work horse and carriage horse.

An old farm wagon.

The Farm Wagon

The wooden-wheeled, horse-drawn farm wagon, used to move heavy and bulky loads, was the precursor of the truck on the farm. Usually, it was a four-wheeled vehicle with a flat bed or a box, having a spring seat to ease the discomfort of the driver and any passengers.

The wagon was pulled by one or more horses, ordinarily by a team of two, and was used for such work as bringing in the crops from the field; hauling livestock, milk, and grain to town; and bringing supplies back. You can still see an occasional old farm wagon being towed by a tractor, although most of them have worn out or been sold to city folk who plant the wooden wheels in their front yard. A special type of wagon, having paddles in the back, was used to spread manure in the fields.

When pulled by a team, the wagon had a long tongue, a doubletree, and two singletrees or whiffletrees to which the horses were hitched.

In addition to the heavier farm wagon, there also was the spring wagon, a smaller and lighter four-wheeled vehicle used to move lighter loads. It usually was drawn by one horse and served about the same purpose the pickup truck does today. There also were other variations of the farm wagon.

Farm cart.

The whifflestrees and doubletree.

Wagon wheel.

A typical carriage.

The Carriage

What the passenger car is today, the horse-drawn carriage was on the American farm before the day of the auto. Having four wheels and two seats, usually with a top, the carriage was the principal family conveyance on the farm. It was drawn by either one or two horses.

Especially in the cities, the carriage sometimes was rather sumptuous, taking such forms as the landau and the phaeton. Around the turn of the century, the carriage served as a sort of status symbol, just as the automobile does today in some circles.

Essentially, however, the carriage was a four-passenger vehicle with a top that could be removed or folded back, equipped with kerosene lamps that often were rather elegant, a whip socket, and a dashboard to keep stones, dirt, and other objectionable matter from being propelled into the front seat.

Fancy carriage lamps.

30

Horse and carriage.

The Carriage Horse

"...we'll hitch old Dobbin to the shay."

The carriage horse, also known as the coach horse and light-harness horse, was a lighter, faster, and more intelligent animal than the work horse. He or she was used to pull carriages, buggies, shays (chaises), surreys, buckboards, runabouts, and similar passenger vehicles.

The carriage horse usually could be trusted to proceed safely down the road without close supervision, in case the driver had other matters on his mind, such as a feminine companion.

These horses often had names, such as "Nellie" or "Prince," and were close to the hearts of their owners.

A surrey with the fringe on top.

The Surrey

"...the surrey with a fringe on top."

The surrey was made so famous by the musical play, *Oklahoma!,* that it deserves special mention, although essentially it was merely a form of two-seated carriage with a top that might or might not have a fringe running around its perimeter.

31

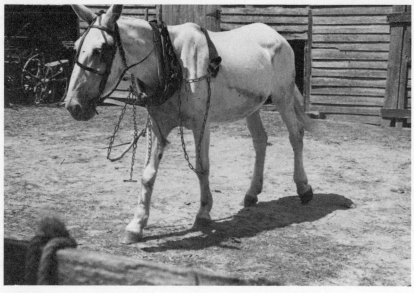

The old gray mare.

The Horse and Buggy

"The old gray mare, she ain't what she used to be."

Farmers sometimes used to saddle a horse when they wanted to visit a friend or make a trip to town, but the usual means of travel for one or two persons was the horse and buggy. The buggy would hold small packages and served the same general purpose that an auto does today, except that it would average only about four to six miles an hour.

The buggy also was the traditional vehicle used when a young man went courting. The farm boy would hitch up the mare to the one-seated buggy that held just two persons, call for his girl friend, take her for a ride about the countryside or to a church social, and then park near some pleasant, secluded spot, just as he does today in his convertible.

A lot of parking was done in the horse-and-buggy days because there were no drive-ins, hamburger stands, bowling alleys, or proper dance halls for young people to patronize in the country.

A buggy.

Successor to the buggy.

A sleigh.

Sleigh bells.

The Sleigh

"Over the river and through the woods
To Grandfather's house we go. . . ."

That couplet from the old jingle
brings back many a fond memory to
folk who were raised on a farm in
the northern part of the country. A
sleigh with its merry bells was found
on every farm.

When the ground was covered with
snow or ice it was much easier for a
horse or a team to pull a vehicle on
runners. So, in wintertime, the horse-
drawn sleigh took the place of the
buggy and carriage, and the sled replaced the farm wagon.

For rides in the sleigh, the farm
family was usually equipped with a
lap robe, earmuffs, wool mittens, and
heavy scarfs, not to mention high
boots and a foot warmer.

33

Privies came single.

—and in pairs.

—and in rows.

The Privy

The privy was the predecessor of the inside bathroom and was standard equipment on every farm. Though still found near farm homes and other rural buildings where there is no running water, the number of privies is steadily shrinking.

Often there were two privies—one for women and one for men. To distinguish between the two, there either were name plates such as you find on public restroom doors today or else symbols, such as a crescent for women and a star for men.

Privies, sometimes called outhouses and various other names, were built in different sizes, commonly known as one-holers, two-holers, and so on. The privy usually was located near, but not too near, the farmhouse, so that it could be reached quickly in bad weather or other emergency.

The privy tends to disappear from the farm soon after electricity and running water are installed, and it isn't hard to see why. The inside bathroom has several advantages over the outdoor privy, including better protection from heat and cold, greater accessibility, greater privacy, and a better all-around atmosphere.

The old farm home.

The Old Farmhouse

The farm home has undergone a continuing evolution. The early settlers were content with a plain one-story log cabin, since the basic requirements were only a roof to keep out rain and sun, walls to keep in the heat in cold weather and keep out wild animals and human intruders, and maybe an inside partition or loft for privacy.

Then, as farm life became less primitive and families grew in size, more comfortable farm homes began to appear. These new homes took on many sizes and shapes, depending on geography and individual taste. Some were so well designed and constructed and so beautiful that many generations have occupied them.

A typical farmhouse was two and a half stories high, with a huge kitchen, a large dining room, a parlor, and several bedrooms. Later a bathroom was added, usually by dividing one of the bedrooms. The attic, or space above the second or third floor, was where the hired man slept unless he had a shack of his own and where old belongings were stored.

The little log cabin.

Farm homes often were square, with a large porch across the front and a smaller porch in back. Many, however, were L-shaped and rectangular; and some which started out as simple rectangles wound up with several additions built to make room for new family members added by birth or marriage. Regardless of shape, these old homes usually were built near shade trees which provided ample protection from sun and wind.

Many of today's younger farm families seem to prefer the one-story house again, similar to the ranch house of the southwest and the rambler of the contemporary suburb.

A few old log cabins and thousands of older farm homes still stand, but many are disintegrating rapidly as the farm population continues to dwindle.

Disintegrating farm house.

Modern farm home.

Kitchen fireplace.

The Kitchen Fireplace

The fireplace in the farm home in the early days was a quite different thing from the living room fireplace of today. It was much bigger and served valuable purposes other than cheering up the room on a cold or damp day.

The farm fireplace was the one source of heat for the early farm home, the place where all of the food was cooked, clothes were dried, and so on.

A typical farm fireplace, located in the kitchen, had a long crane on which hung one or more iron kettles for cooking. A bellows usually rested nearby to help encourage the fire.

Later on, the kitchen fireplace was supplemented and then replaced by various types of stoves, each with its own coal scuttle or wood box, and smaller fireplaces were built in various other rooms as the house expanded. Some farm homes had eight or ten individual fireplaces in bedrooms and elsewhere before central heating was introduced. Labor and fuel both were cheaper in those days.

The flames in those large old kitchen fireplaces could get mighty hot and bright when a large fire was burning. To protect the faces of family members who were huddled close to the fire to keep warm on cold winter days, the farm home often had one or more face screens, made of wood and pivoted so they could be adjusted to any direction or height.

38

The coal scuttle.

A face screen.

An early coal stove.

An iron range.

The Iron Range

The big iron range was an early type of farm kitchen stove. It burned either wood or coal, usually wood which was plentiful and free on almost any farm. The range had four or more openings in its flat surface over which pots and pans were placed. Covering the openings were iron lids which could be removed with the aid of a special lifter.

The iron range also had an oven for baking and roasting and several compartments for keeping food warm. Lacking insulation of any kind, the iron range was a source of considerable heat, whether wanted or not, thus giving rise to the expression, "Slaving over a hot stove," which modern housewives often mention as a reason for wanting to eat out or else serve a cold meal.

The Dry Sink

The task of washing dishes often was accomplished in what was called a dry sink, shaped somewhat like today's sink but made of wood with a metal lining. There was a drain in the bottom so the dishwater could empty into a slop jar placed below.

The sink was filled with hot water from a pail that had been set on the stove or in the fireplace to heat.

Wooden icebox.

A dry sink.

The Wooden Icebox

The wooden icebox, later available in metal, was one of the first great additions to the farm kitchen after the iron range. The icebox took several forms—a horizontal box with shelves inside and a lid that lifted up or a larger, vertical box with several doors and compartments, one for the ice and the others for perishable foods.

A 25-pound block of ice would last a whole day or longer if the doors were not opened too often. The melting ice drained into a pan that had to be emptied regularly or into a pipe that led outside through the wall.

The farm boy or his father went to the icehouse whenever necessary to fetch another block of ice from its sawdust nest. Nowadays, of course, there's an electric refrigerator in almost every farm home.

Vertical phone.

The Hand-Crank Telephone

Because farms were so scattered, their early telephone service was furnished via party-line over which a dozen or more families received their calls. Each family had a separate ring so they could tell whether an incoming call was for them or for someone else. Two short rings meant one subscriber, a long and a short meant someone else, and so on.

To initiate a call, you first listened on your wall-hung, party-line phone to make sure it was not in use and then you turned the small crank at the side of the phone to notify the operator that you wanted to make a call. You also turned the crank when you had completed the call to inform the operator, known as "Central," that you were through.

Busy as farm life was, the farmer and his wife frequently found time to listen in on every call that came through, regardless of who was being called. If the call concerned a matter of general interest, such as ripe gossip or scandal, there might be a large number of people listening in.

Today, party-line service is more private, and the old wall-hung phone with the crank is getting to be as hard to find as a work ox. It was replaced by the vertical phone with separate mouthpiece and receiver, which in turn gave way to today's models.

Party-line phone.

42

Do-it-yourself candles.

A candlestick.

The Candle Mold

Whether for reasons of economy, necessity, or convenience, farmers made for themselves in the old days many articles that they buy in stores today. Among those articles were candles, which before the day of kerosene were the principal source of artificial light. Abe Lincoln did much of his extensive reading by candlelight.

The candles were made by the farm wife in special molds, using tallow instead of the paraffin commonly used in store-bought candles.

In addition to the vertical candlestick and the candelabrum found today in many homes, every household had a candlestick shaped like a saucer, with a small handle for carrying lighted candles about the house and lighting the way up to bed at night.

43

A canopy bed.

The Canopy Bed

The large four-poster canopy bed was the pride and joy of the master bedroom in any farm or town home. The purpose of the posts was to support a top from which hung curtains which could be drawn to afford both privacy and warmth. Many of these fine beds were elaborately carved and handsomely decorated with silk and lace.

The sleeping surface of the canopy, or tester, bed usually was so high that steps were required to enter it.

The warmth provided by the top and curtains became less necessary with the advent of central heating and, since privacy could be achieved in other ways, the canopy bed began to go out of style, except in homes where antiques are valued highly and the past is held dear.

The truth is that the canopy bed is too costly, too hard to make up, too difficult to get into, and too large for the average home today.

The Bed Steps

The bed steps needed to climb into a canopy bed also served other purposes. For one thing, they could be used in libraries to help reach books on high shelves.

More importantly, a thundermug often was kept under the top step, which was hinged, and the whole affair then served as a toilet for use in emergencies.

There usually were three steps in a bed steps.

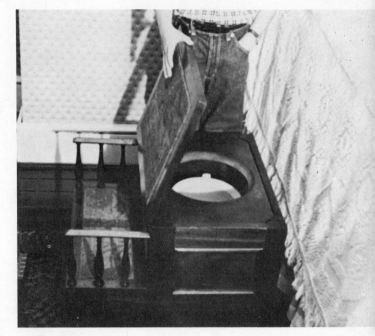

Open top step.

A trundle bed.

The Trundle Bed

Referred to also as a truckle bed, the trundle bed was a small, low bed which could be rolled under a larger bed in the daytime. The smaller bed was used by young children so they could be close to their parents during the night or by young slaves or apprentices whose masters wanted them nearby.

The trundle bed was both shorter and narrower, as well as lower, than the adult bed under which it was rolled when not in use. These days, parents and employers usually want to be away from their children and employees when they sleep, so the trundle bed now is a curiosity.

Woolen and cylindrical foot warmers.

The Foot Warmer

Before we had automatic heat, electric blankets, and car heaters, the foot warmer in its various forms was an indispensable item of family equipment.

One type of foot warmer consisted of a long-handled, covered pan containing hot coals, which was inserted between the sheets of a bed on cold nights. Its purpose, obviously, was to eliminate cold feet which were inevitable, for at least a few minutes, when retiring in an unheated bedroom.

Foot warmers also were taken to church and used to keep warm in sleighs and carriages in wintertime. Some took the form of metal boxes and cylinders into which live coals could be placed; others were heated stones with handles and wrapped in blankets, and some consisted merely of woolen bags into which the feet could be inserted.

Box foot warmer.

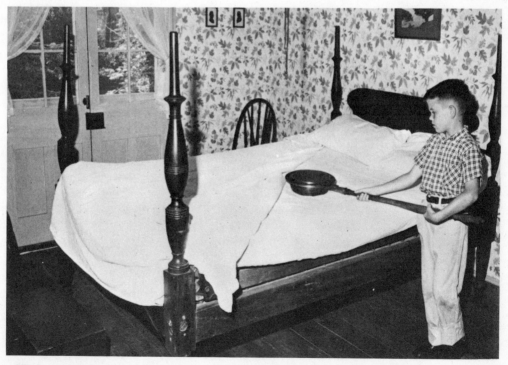

Warming pan.

A thundermug.

The Thundermug

This object can be remembered without too much trouble from one's early days. Today it is known as a pottie and is used principally to toilet-train young children. It used to be called a thundermug or chamber pot or comfort pot. It was kept under the bed for emergency use when it was not convenient to visit the privy. Often the thundermug had a lid, such as the one shown under the bed.

The thundermug has been replaced where there is running water by a water closet or toilet, the first of which had an overhead tank which was tripped by pulling on a chain.

Pull-chain toilet.

Pottie chair.

48

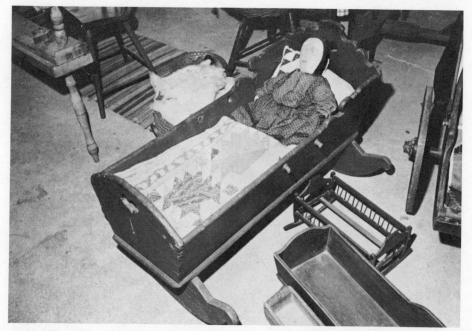

Small cradle.

The Cradle

"Rockabye baby in the tree top.
When the wind blows, the cradle will rock.
When the bough breaks, the cradle will fall.
Down will come cradle, baby and all."

Cradles already are collectors' items, yet once the cradle was as indispensable a part of the farm home as the hand pump and the thundermug. Every young baby was raised in a cradle, where it could be gently rocked to and fro with the aid of a fond mother's foot.

Today, rocking is deemed unnecessary, so the baby is placed in a bassinet, which usually is on wheels so it can be rolled about the house, or in a car basket so the child can be taken along when parents go shopping or visiting.

A washstand.

The Pitcher and Basin

Washing your face and hands hasn't always been as convenient as it is today. On the farm, in the days before running water, you used a basin which you filled from a pitcher, both being kept on a wooden stand along with a soap dish. The pitcher had to be filled at the pump, and the basin was emptied after use into a slop jar which, in turn, had to be carried outside for emptying.

Most farms also had a basin outside near the pump for use by hired hands and others who did not care to go inside.

Naturally, since there was so much pumping and carrying required to supply fresh water, people tended to use it conservatively, but with practice you could get reasonably clean even so.

The washstand in the modern farm home is in the bathroom.

Galvanized tub.

The Saturday Night Bath

Gone forever is another tradition of the farm—the weekly Saturday night bath. Of course, members of farm families still bathe on Saturdays but they now bathe on other days, as well.

Considering the chore of carrying water from the pump, heating it on the stove, and then carrying it out again after the bath, it is no wonder that one bath a week was considered sufficient on many farms in the old days. Saturday night was chosen because people wanted to be nice and clean for church on Sunday and, in the case of younger folk, for the Saturday night date.

With no bathtub or running water available, the bathing was done in a large wooden or galvanized washtub which in cold weather was placed near the stove or fireplace in the kitchen. In summer the tub could be used outside if privacy were not a factor.

Smaller members of the family often were bathed several at a time to conserve water.

Today, more and more farms have a bathroom, with the necessary facilities, so it is an easy matter to bathe much more frequently than just on Saturday night. And there no longer is any reason to expect more than one individual to use a tubful of water.

51

Wooden tub.

The Kerosene Lamp

One of the usual daily chores for the farm boy and girl was taking care of the kerosene lamps—filling them with kerosene, trimming the wicks, and cleaning the glass chimneys. Kerosene lamps were widely used before electricity reached the farm and gave out far more light than the candles they displaced.

Each farm was equipped with one or more of these lamps and, if the number of lamps was limited or if no light was burning upstairs, a lamp was taken up to the bedroom when the family retired at night. Some of the kerosene lamps were quite ornate, and many have been saved and converted to electricity for use in present-day homes. In larger homes, there was a chandelier or a large kerosene lamp hanging from the ceiling.

In addition to kerosene lamps, the farmer also had kerosene lanterns for use outdoors and in barns after dark. The great Chicago fire of 1871 has been attributed to flames started when a cow kicked over a kerosene lantern while being milked. The lantern has been replaced on the farm by the electric lamp or flashlight.

Kerosene lamp.

A chandelier.

52

Leaching tubs.

Making Soap

Soap is another essential item that formerly was made on the farm, whereas today it is purchased in food stores and drugstores.

The principal ingredients in farm soap were tallow and lye. Tallow was obtained by melting the fat of cattle and sheep, while the lye was produced by leaching wood ashes.

Ashes from fireplaces and stoves were collected in a stone ashpit, usually located in the basement of the farm home. When a sufficient supply of ashes had been collected, they were leached in water in special tubs kept for that purpose.

Churn with plunger.

Churn with crank.

The Butter Churn

Making butter was a regular chore on almost every farm in the old days. It was made from fresh cream, and the churn was operated by hand, usually with the help of the farm boy if his mother could find him. (There were countless ways of keeping farm children productively occupied in those days.)

Although an electrically operated churn eventually came onto the market, the early churns were powered either by turning a crank, working a plunger up and down, or rocking with a foot.

With so many other things to do today, farm wives buy their butter in town, along with their other groceries, instead of bothering to make it themselves.

Lard kettle.

The Lard Kettle

With high-quality lard now available in handy one-pound cartons at any food store and with vegetable shortening in widespread use, the practice of making lard on the farm is fast disappearing. Consequently, the large iron kettles once used to render or clarify hog fat and to make tallow are rusting away or else serving ornamental purposes.

Lard was made at butchering time, usually by the farm wife with the aid of any available male help. The process consisted of melting and rendering the fat of hogs over a hot wood fire, usually out of doors. The kettle hung from a tripod and rested on the logs, or else was placed on a special fireplace built for that purpose.

Carders.

Carding Wool

Before wool or other fiber could be spun into yarn, it had to be disentangled and straightened. For that purpose, farm wives used carders—flat boards or paddles with short, slender spikes protruding on one side.

Carding consisted of placing the wool between the two paddles and moving them to and fro. Carding wool was another way to pass the after-dinner hours on the farm before the days of radio and television.

Large spinning wheel.

Small spinning wheel.

The Spinning Wheel

Our great-grandmothers and some of our grandmothers, too, were very busy women if they lived on a farm. In addition to feeding, bathing, and dressing the children, milking a few cows, churning the butter, making candles, baking bread and cake and pies, putting up preserves, and canning vegetables, they used to make their own thread and yarn on a spinning wheel.

The larger spinning wheel was turned by hand, while the smaller wheel was operated by a treadle. Spinning wheels of every size are collectors' items today because farm women have become emancipated, just like city women only not quite so much. Farm wives now use factory-made thread for mending and buy factory-made clothes for the family.

A clock reel.

The Loom

After carding and spinning, there remains the task of weaving the cloth. Weaving requires a loom, which may be relatively simple, like those used on the old-time farm, or really complicated such as the ones used in modern factories.

The farm loom was operated by foot power and took a fair amount of skill. The task of operating it usually fell to the farm wife or an older daughter or perhaps grandma.

Two aids for the weaver were the clock reel and the swift. The clock reel was used both to measure the yarn and to form it into hanks or loops, while the swift was a device for winding the yarn preparatory to spinning.

The hand loom.

A swift.

58

A grindstone.

The Grindstone

When you want to sharpen a knife or axe or any other kind of tool today, you turn on the electrically powdered grinder, but in the early days you used a grindstone which was powered either by hand or by treadle.

Farm with a windmill.

The Windmill

Take a good look at the next windmill you see as you drive about the countryside because, at the rate they are rusting away, windmills will be almost impossible to find in a few more years. Yet until the late 1930's, when electric power began to reach more and more farms, the windmill was just as vital to the farm as the work horse ever had been. It was the dominant feature of the rural skyline, along with the majestic oak and maple and the thin column of smoke from the farm chimney.

The windmill was the principal source of water for farm homes and farm animals alike, often running day and night to fill troughs and tanks with precious water pumped from the ground. Windmills also were used to grind grain where water power was not available, and they performed other valuable functions.

Nowadays, the electric pump has replaced the windmill on most farms because it can be depended on to provide water even when there isn't enough wind to operate a windmill. Where there is no electricity, and sometimes when there is, the farm pump is operated by a gasoline engine.

The mechanically driven pump has replaced the windmill as a source of water, and on the long rural horizon the windmill has been replaced by the television aerial. On some farms, in fact, the television aerial has been mounted on the very same tower that formerly supported the windmill. The two serve entirely different purposes, but it is an interesting coincidence that the new use for the tower came along just as the other was disappearing.

A Cape Cod windmill.

Replacement for the windmill.

Also prominent on the farm skyline now is the utility pole that brings to the farm the electricity that operates the television and replaces the windmill.

The covered well.

The Well

Many farms had an open well from which they obtained clear, cold water by lowering a bucket on the end of a rope or chain. Wells often were covered by a roof to shelter anyone using them in inclement weather and also to keep foreign objects from falling in. But accidents sometimes happened, as described in the old nursery rhyme:

> "Ding, dong, dell
> Pussy's in the well. . . ."

Perishable foods, such as milk, cream, butter, and eggs, were lowered into the well in a bucket or pail to keep them fresh as long as possible in the cold water.

The coming of electricity and mechanical refrigeration eliminated the need for open wells, but some farmers keep them in service anyhow, just for old time's sake.

The old oaken bucket.

Wooden pump.

A pump house.

The Hand Pump

In the good old days when you wanted a pail of water for the kitchen stove or the washstand, you went out to the hand pump and pumped the water from a well in the ground, unless you preferred to use an open well. Today, of course, you turn a faucet and the electric or gasoline pump does the work for you. The faucet is a real improvement because pumping was hard work. It is easy to see why people used water more sparingly in those days.

Pumping up one or two pails of water wasn't too much of a job for the farm boy, to whom the work usually was entrusted. But, when the windmill wasn't working and he needed to fill a large trough for the livestock, that pump handle could get mighty heavy and, on a cold day, his fingers could get pretty stiff.

The main hand pump often was located in a pump house under the windmill, sheltered from the elements. The modern tendency is to locate the pump and motor in the basement of the farm home or in some other nearby building.

63

Hand milking.

Milking the Cows

This chore isn't as easy as it might look. To milk a cow by hand, you not only need to know how to make the milk come out and in the right direction, but you also need to know how to keep the cow from kicking you and knocking the pail of milk across the barn.

Hand-milking is a thing of the past on most farms, especially the big commercial dairy farms that use electric milking machines to reduce labor costs. Of course, the farmer who milks one or two cows for his own family use can't afford a milking machine, so there still is some hand-milking. But it is a dying art as more and more farmers buy their milk in town. That milk is likely to be cleaner and more healthful and is a lot less work.

Farm boys never did care too much about milking because it came at bad times: early in the morning before breakfast when the boy was hungry and still sleepy and then again in the afternoon when he also was hungry and beginning to be a bit tired after a hard day's work.

Cider press.

The Cider Press

Almost every northern farm had one or more apple trees, and many farmers either owned or borrowed a press with which to make cider for home consumption, if not for sale. The apples were pressed or squeezed in the fall of the year when they became ripe and juicy. The cider usually was consumed shortly after it was made, although the juice sometimes was allowed to harden until it developed an alcoholic content.

In addition, when distilled or frozen, cider turned into a brandy known as applejack, which was highly regarded by some countryfolk.

Making cider was one job that wasn't foisted off on the farm boy. His elders generally preferred to do the work themselves so as to make sure it was done right. The accidental inclusion of a rotten or wormy apple could alter the flavor of a whole batch of cider or applejack. Nowadays, most farmers buy their cider at a store.

Scarecrow.

The Scarecrow

Another once familiar sight you will miss the next time you drive through the rural countryside is the scarecrow, formerly used by most farmers to scare birds away from the farm garden and the crops, especially the corn.

The scarecrow generally was made of castoff garments and hung on a crossbar in such a way as to resemble a human figure. It would wave in the breeze and supposedly frighten the birds.

Scarecrows went out of fashion even before farm gardens started to diminish in numbers, because it was decided that they didn't accomplish their purpose. Their disappearance makes one wonder what will become of the expression, "She looked like a scarecrow," as applied to a dowdily dressed female. Members of the younger generation who never have seen a scarecrow will hardly grasp the full significance of the term.

Haystacks.

The Haystack

"... and the little boy who looks after the sheep
is under the haystack, fast asleep."

When farmers used to stack their surplus hay in the field until it was
needed in the barn, the countryside was often dotted with haystacks. But
that was before the day of the modern machines which either cut the
hay and place it in a truck body for delivery to a silo or else cut and bale
the hay, all in one operation.

You've heard about the man who undertook the almost impossible job
of finding a needle in a haystack. Today in most localities it is even harder
to find a haystack.

Disappearing along with the haystack is the flatbed wagon onto which
the hay was loaded, either by pitchfork or by mechanical loader, for hauling to the stack or the barn.

The haystack was a favorite spot for farm youngsters to romp and relax,
and their elders, too, often chose the stack as a place to recline, alone or
accompanied.

A hay loader.

The Pitchfork.

The old hay wagon.

The Threshing Machine

A startling sight on the farm horizon in early summer used to be the cloud of thick black smoke from the coal-fired steam engine that provided power for the threshing machine during the grain harvest.

But the smoke cloud is vanishing, not only because a gasoline or diesel tractor has replaced the smoking steam engine, but also because the combine that cuts and threshes the grain in one operation is fast crowding out the threshing machine, just as the binder replaced the cradle in the harvesting operation.

A grain cradle.

Leaving the scene along with the steam engine, the threshing machine, and the binder which cut the grain and tied it into bundles with the aid of binder twine, are the golden shocks that used to dot the countryside briefly each summer between the time the wheat or other grain was cut and the day it was threshed. Instead of forming bundles of grain to be collected by hand and piled into shocks, the combine pours the grain into bags and throws the straw out on the ground to be raked into rows and picked up by a machine that bales it like hay.

The combine, operated by two men, also eliminates the large threshing crew, composed of the farmer and his neighbors (and their hired men). Gone, too, are the bountiful lunches which the farm wives prepared and served to the ravenous crew when the threshing machine came to their farms.

A grain binder.

Shocking wheat.

The threshing machine.

The steam engine that ran the threshing machine.

A new-fangled combine.

Corn shocks.

The Corn Shock

Modern mechanical advancement also has doomed another farm standby —the corn shocks that stood in the fields like sentinels after harvest, an unmistakable sign that summer was gone and fall had arrived for sure. Unlike the smaller wheat shocks that remained in the fields only a few days, the corn shocks often stood there well into the winter, until hauled to the barnyard to serve as fodder for the livestock.

Passing, too, is the hand-picking of corn, for the work now is done by machine. This means an end to the traditional corn-picking contests and the corn-husking bees that used to enliven farm life in the fall of the year when the apples were ripe and the cider was fresh from the press.

Corn sheller.

The Corn Sheller

Any tenderfoot who couldn't harness horses or milk cows could at least make himself useful on the farm by operating a corn sheller, which required no skill but needed quite a bit of elbow grease. Shelling corn took a lot of time and energy when there were numerous young animals to be fed, and a boy's arm could get mighty tired.

The purpose of the sheller was to remove the kernels of corn from the cob, making the corn easier for the colt or calf or chickens to eat. Nowadays the same result is accomplished by mechanical means, thus freeing the farm boy for other more important work such as cleaning out a carburetor or changing a tire.

Pile of wood.

The Woodpile

Sawing logs and splitting them into firewood used to be major chores on the farm but not today. Cooking now is done for the most part with electricity or bottled gas, and the farm home is heated with fuel oil, so the woodpile has lost the essentiality it once enjoyed.

The farmer who has any sawing to be done these days either owns or borrows a power saw that will do the job with less human effort and much faster. The circular saw which can be run off the back wheel of a truck was the first substitute for elbow grease before the advent of the chain saw.

The crosscut saw and the bucksaw, that once gave the farm boy so much exercise on cold winter days, are now hanging on a nail in the barn, and the sharp axe seldom gets a workout.

Rail fence.

The Rail Fence

The rail fence, made famous by Abe Lincoln, the rail splitter, is another element of early farm life that is fast becoming hard to find. Splitting rails from large logs was a man-sized job but the cheapest way of fencing a farm if logs were plentiful.

Most farm fences today are made of posts and boards or metal wire or mesh. Barbed wire and electric current both are used to discourage fence climbing.

Mending fences used to be a traditional cold-weather chore on every farm where rails were used.

Board fence.

A stile.

The Stile

When you want to get on the other side of a fence and there is no gate handy, you can jump over, climb over, crawl under, crawl through, or detour. It isn't hard to climb a plain board fence but getting over a barbed wire fence can cause you real trouble.

The best way to get over a fence without damage, if there is no gate, is with the aid of a stile. However, stiles are becoming hard to find because you can't take a truck or tractor over a stile, and that is the way farmers do most of their traveling these days. Walking is just about out of style on a farm.

New farm pond.

The Old Swimming Hole

Usually a wide or deep place in a creek, the old swimming hole where farm boys and girls had so much unregulated fun may never disappear entirely. Swimming holes, however, are becoming less numerous every year as cities and towns encroach on the countryside and various substitutes spring up.

Most farms now have a pond which serves as a swimming pool, a place for boating and fishing, and an emergency water supply. Then, too, most communities now have fancy swimming pools that are safer, more convenient, and perhaps more sanitary than the old swimming hole.

The latter lacked a bathhouse in which to change clothes, if swimming attire was to be worn, and had no showers, lifeguard, or towels, but it was much more informal and there weren't nearly as many rules to worry about.

Old swimming hole.

Walking to school.

Walking to School

Among the many rigors of early farm life was the necessity for walking to school. Since rural schools were few in number as well as small in size, owing to the low density of farm population, some youngsters had to walk a mile or more each way to school and back, often through rain and snow and cold. Some walked as far as three or four miles each way, while others rode on horseback or were delivered and called for by horse and buggy.

The distance walked tends to become longer as the ex-students advance in years, because a long walk to school has come to be recognized as a sort of badge of courage and character.

Today the school bus transports the student to and from school. Thus, one more hardship of farm life is disappearing.

One-room school.

The One-Room Schoolhouse

Because there were so few farm children, the one-room schoolhouse, known also as the Little Red Schoolhouse, was ample in many places. All grades were taught by one teacher, and somehow it worked out rather well. At least, some of our most eminent national leaders obtained their early schooling in that way and are very proud of it.

Today, any such arrangement is completely inadequate. In most places, any one-room schoolhouses that still stand have long since been converted to other uses, perhaps rented to families seeking low-cost housing and low taxes.

Instead of one room and one teacher and a dozen pupils, the modern rural school may have as many as 100 rooms and up to 2,000 pupils. Some of the schools occupy as many as forty acres of ground. It isn't uncommon to see a fleet of a dozen or more school buses gathered to take the children home in the afternoon. Things really have changed.

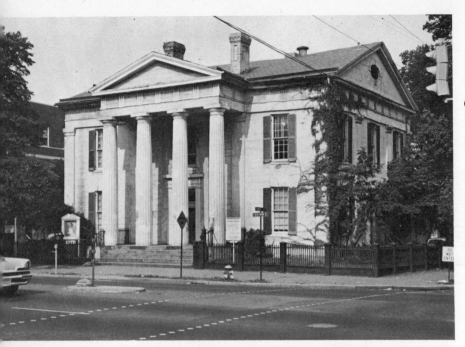

Old family home.

2. Our Changing Homes

Remodeling older homes has become a major new industry in this country. The best home of 1900, sound and well-built as it may be, simply is an impossible place in which to live, by today's standards, until it has been extensively renovated and re-equipped.

The changes in our household equipment have been prodigious as the American family has eagerly sought greater comfort, convenience, and freedom from manual labor. In the town house, as on the farm, electricity has greatly lessened the drudgery of everyday life, especially for the housewife, which is most important in view of the difficulty of finding household help and the high wages it commands.

We hear a great deal about the good old days back home but few, indeed, are the people who would give up their present-day conveniences for the graceful but far less convenient days of old. Those big old parlors and wide verandas were mighty nice but so are today's family room and outdoor patio. And nostalgia becomes still less acute when oldsters look around at their automatic marvels—thermostatically controlled heat (which requires no labor or attention except the turning of a dial), the dishwasher, garbage disposer, clothes washer, clothes dryer, and air conditioner, to mention a few.

Old home used as funeral parlor.

The Large Town House

Grandfather's pride and joy was the spacious and gracious family home on Main Street or Maple Avenue, conveniently located just a short distance from the heart of downtown. There was living at its best, with large airy rooms, high ceilings, a broad winding staircase leading up to the bedrooms, shuttered windows, and all the rest—on a wide, deep lot with half a dozen huge elms or poplars shading the roof and yard.

Unless the new superhighway has been cut through the yard, the chances are the old home still stands, but there is little likelihood that it still is a private residence and, even if it is, its days are numbered. For one thing, the old home is too big and too costly to operate for the families of today. Moreover, taxes are getting higher every year and close-in land is urgently needed for new stores and municipal parking lots.

And if it does still stand, the old home may have been converted into a funeral parlor or an Elk's Club, or maybe a tea room or rooming house.

Front gate.

The Old Wooden Gate

The wooden gate in the white board fence that ran around the yard back home figured prominently in everyday life. The fence was built in the first place because it looked nice or it restrained pedestrians from taking shortcuts through the yard or it kept young children from wandering away or it fenced in a vicious or valuable dog. The gate also provided access to the house.

In addition, the gate was a favorite place for children to play, swinging back and forth as they stood on the bottom rail, thus inviting reprimands from parents who feared the hinges of the gate would be loosened.

The gate also was likely to disappear temporarily on Halloween, the victim of innocent pranksters in the days before such antics were classed as juvenile delinquency.

Finally, the old front gate was the place where the young boy said his lingering goodbye or goodnight to his current girl friend before they became old enough for a goodnight kiss at the front door or in the vestibule.

Front porch.

The Front Porch

The substantial home in town or city, or on the farm, was not complete without its wide front porch, also known as a veranda. Here the family relaxed on warm evenings and Sunday afternoons, watching the passers-by; and the young people used to spoon after dark when lights were low.

Usually, but not always, the front porch had a railing on which the men-folk could put their feet and enjoy solid comfort and where one could sit if all the chairs were occupied. The front porch was equipped with various types of chairs, including rockers, and generally had a swinging settee suspended by means of chains from hooks in the ceiling. The chains almost always creaked.

Some front porches were screened to afford protection from flies and mosquitos, and some were fitted with storm windows so the space could be utilized in cold weather. That led to the practice of permanently enclosing the porch with siding and windows or louvers, thus providing an additional room for year-around use.

The successor to the front porch, of course, is the patio, which instead of being out front is in the back where the family can relax in a much more informal manner than was deemed proper in front. Now Dad can demonstrate the gentle art of barbecuing, and everyone can indulge in sun bathing. All that's left of the front porch on the modern home is the small stoop where you wait for the door to open.

Swinging settee.

Cupola.

Widow's walk.

The Cupola

In the Victorian era and for some years after, it was fashionable to build houses that were ornamental as well as functional. Among the more popular forms of ornamentation were the cupola and various curves, points, and squares that sometimes resembled dentures and often were referred to as gingerbread.

The cupola was a graceful cone placed above the roofline, usually as an ornamentation, but on some homes it also took the form of a lookout, called a widow's walk. It took that name because it enabled the wife of a sea captain to watch for the return or non-return of her husband's ship from faraway ports. This lookout sometimes was a fenced platform on the roof, rather than being an enclosure.

In this day of overseas telephone, radio, and cable, news of the movements of a ship or disaster at sea is transmitted so quickly that there no longer is need for a widow's walk.

The same type of cupola also was found on homes located many miles from the seacoast, presumably because it was thought to make the house more attractive.

Inside shutters and venetian blinds.

The Inside Shutters

Regulating the amount of light and air that enters the windows of a home has been a problem through the years. Prior to the introduction of the window shade and its temperamental roller and the more recent venetian blind, one early solution was the inside shutter, which could be adjusted to admit some light and air, or none at all, or could be swung back to leave the window unobstructed.

The hatrack.

The Hatrack

Even the grandest of our early homes lacked many present-day essentials, and one of them is the front-hall closet where members of the family and guests can leave their belongings when entering the home.

Consequently, unless there was a butler to stow things away, each home had to have a hatrack, either in the kitchen or just inside the front door, plus an umbrella stand to hold umbrellas, canes, parasols, and the like. The latter usually was placed under or near the hatrack.

The front-hall closet serves both of these purposes today and others besides, since it may hold the vacuum cleaner, golf clubs, tennis rackets, ice and roller skates, galoshes and rubbers, telephone books, and other miscellaneous items as well as hats and outerwear.

The hatrack usually was square or oblong in shape, with a mirror in the center.

An umbrella stand.

Grandfather clock.

The Grandfather Clock

One of the finer possessions in our early homes was the grandfather clock, tall and impressive, usually found in a parlor or front hall, sometimes on the landing between the first and second floors in a large home.

It had a pendulum with weights, and it struck the hour and half-hour. It had to be wound by hand which, aside from the cost, may be one reason why the electric clock and the clock radio have taken over in most modern homes.

The grandfather clock was so highly prized by many families that it remained in place as a decorative piece and reminder of the past long after it had ceased telling time.

Nicknacks and whatnot.

The Whatnot

Housewives always have needed a place to keep and display bric-a-brac, objets d'art, souvenirs, curios, and whatnot. To accommodate such items, a piece of furniture was invented and named a whatnot. It contained a number of shelves on which miscellaneous objects could be placed and varied in height from five to eight feet or more and from three to six feet in width. Sometimes it contained a mirror which, among other things, permitted two views of each object.

As room sizes began to shrink, due to the increased cost of building and servant shortages, whatnots have been de-emphasized. Today, the objects that once appeared on them are found on small tables, hanging shelves, and similar items.

The Tea Caddy

Prior to the introduction of the tea-bag, it was fashionable to have a tea caddy. The tea caddy contained compartments in which tea and sugar could be kept and a glass container into which the used leaves could be dumped prior to making a fresh batch of the beverage.

A tea caddy would be equally useful today in disposing of used teabags, but it really isn't necessary if you don't mind putting the limp, dripping bag on the side of your saucer after it has served its purpose.

A tea caddy.

A music box.

The Music Box

Back when the types of recreation available in the home and elsewhere were far less numerous than they are today, the music box was one means of entertaining the family and friends. Preceding the talking machine and phonograph, music boxes played several types of metallic records. The assortment, though, was limited and the volume of sound was restrained, while the tone left something to be desired.

89

A pump organ.

The Pump Organ

The pump organ was a proud possession of many a farm or town family with a member talented enough to play it. Used for playing favorite hymns as well as classical and popular pieces, the pump organ helped to provide inspiration and entertainment for the family during the long evening hours and on Sunday.

Oft-repeated pieces were: "Rock of Ages," "Then I'll Remember You," "I've Been Working on the Railroad," and "The Girl I Loved in Tennessee."

The more elaborate pump organs also doubled as whatnots for the display of photographs, nicknacks, vases, trophies, and the like.

Upright piano.

Piano stool.

The Player Piano

The upright piano around which the family used to gather to sing hymns, Christmas carols, favorite classics, and the latest ragtime—the piano that used to play the cops-and-robbers music at the neighborhood movie theater —the piano that was the center of attention at young peoples' parties in the olden days—the piano around which the barbershop quartette originated —has given way to the spinet, the concert grand, and other modern models, but the memory lingers on.

The player piano, an upright equipped to play perforated music rolls by pumping foot pedals, was equally popular, especially with young people who had limited musical talents but possessed strong leg muscles.

A companion to the old upright was the piano stool, the height of which could be varied by twirling the round seat mounted on a spiral rod. It generally had four legs and glass feet. Its successor, the piano bench, lacks the advantage of adjustable height, but contains space to store music and will hold two people, which the stool would not.

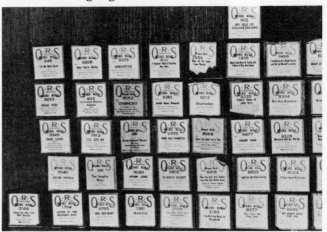

Piano rolls.

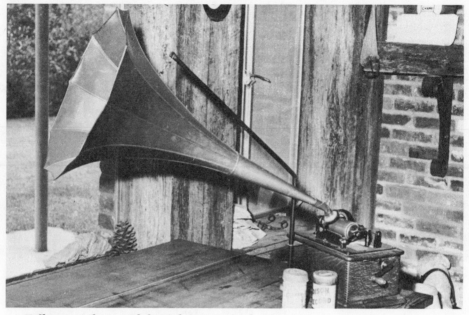

Talking machine with large horn.

The Talking Machine

The most famous of the early talking machines played hollow wax records or cylinders and had a tin horn to amplify the sound. There was a choice of singing, talking, and instrumental selections and a wide variety of titles appeared. Some of the most popular were: "Onward, Christian Soldiers," "Way Down Yonder in the Corn Field," "My Old Kentucky Home," "Stars and Stripes Forever," and "Sweet Adeline."

The early talking machine had to be wound with a crank or key after a few records, as did its first successor, the phonograph, which eliminated the horn in favor of a more compact speaker and had a turntable that played flat discs.

It wasn't long, however, before that blessing known as electricity replaced the hand crank and then other refinements appeared, including the automatic record-changer and stereophonic high fidelity.

The high-fidelity music now available unquestionably has better tone and quality than its predecessors, but the old talking machine with its tin horn was responsible for many happy hours as young people, and their parents, too, listened or danced to the old-time tunes.

Talking machine with small horn.

Phonograph.

A stereoscope.

The Stereoscope

In the days when there was no such entertainment as movies, color-slide projectors, picture magazines, and television, the stereoscope was a popular source of education and good, clean fun in many homes. A well-supplied parlor had a wide range of double photographs showing scenery, history, and art mounted on cards, which gave the impression of depth when seen through the special viewer.

Favorite subjects, such as the Grand Canyon, Pikes Peak, the Civil War, and the Gibson Girl, were viewed over and over and were helpful in entertaining guests when conversation began to lag or when one wanted an excuse to sit close to a friend.

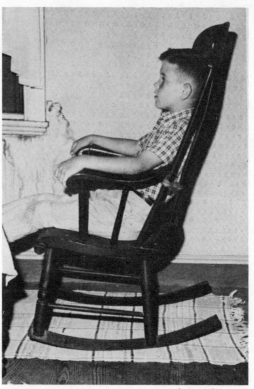

A rocking chair.

The Rocking Chair

You generally associate rocking chairs with mothers rocking their children or grandmothers rocking away as they knit and reminisce. You still find rocking chairs in everyday use but the number grows steadily smaller as stationary upholstered chairs take over, along with occasional chairs, pull-up chairs, contour chairs, and so on.

Today, mothers put their children in cribs, bassinets, or playpens, because modern science says you should just put the child down and leave him alone when the time comes to rest or sleep.

Another reason for the decline of the rocking chair is that it isn't easy to play bridge or canasta or watch television while rocking. Too, so many living rooms and bedrooms are so small that there isn't room for chairs which have a limited purpose. There was a day, though, and not so long ago, when you couldn't find a home worthy of the name that didn't have at least one rocker and probably a platform rocker.

The Morris chair with its adjustable back was an early attempt to gain the benefits of the contour chair and it, too, is in the antique shop.

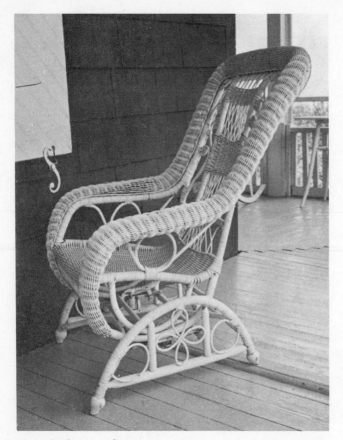

A platform rocker.

Morris chair.

The Foot-Powered Sewing Machine

Remember when sewing machines, like the loom, the spinning wheel, the corn sheller, and the grindstone, were operated by foot-power? That was a lot better than having nothing but a needle and thread, but it was work, even so.

Many of those old machines still remain, but the up-to-date model operated by our old friend, electricity, saves milady's energy for other essential household duties.

Feather duster.

Old sewing machine.

The Feather Duster

Once found in every home, the feather duster is seldom seen these days except in an occasional store where it is used to dust cans, bottles, and packages.

Even there, a vacuum cleaner or rag is considered more sanitary and efficient since the duster merely moves the dust from one place to another, whereas the more modern methods actually remove the dust.

The Carpet Beater

Every home today has an electrically operated vacuum cleaner to pick up dust and clean rugs and carpets, but it wasn't always so easy. Young boys used to have many ways to keep in good physical condition and one of those ways consisted of taking the rugs and carpets out on the grass or the clothesline and beating them vigorously with a carpet beater made of fiber or wire.

Beating the rugs was a regular chore every month or so, or whenever Mother got the idea that they were getting dirty.

When propelled by a strong right arm, a carpet beater produced a cloud of dust, especially if the chore had been neglected overly long, so it was well to stay on the windward side to avoid suffocation. The job wasn't properly finished until the beating no longer produced dust, and Mother would keep a sharp watch through the kitchen window to make sure the job wasn't being shirked.

One early replacement for the carpet beater was the hand-operated vacuum cleaner, but that never really caught on, perhaps because it was almost as much work as the carpet beater. Eventually the electric vacuum cleaner appeared, and you can find mature people today who say they never heard of a carpet beater.

The hand-operated vacuum-cleaner.

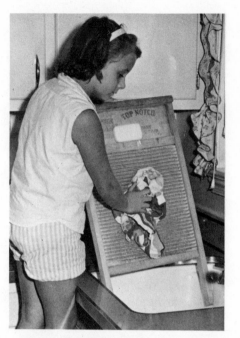

Washing clothes.

Hand-powered washer.

The Washboard

Until the washing machine came along, one piece of equipment found in every home was the washboard. A washboard unquestionably shortened the life of any garment but it did its assigned job, provided it was used with proper energy. There was no surer way of developing a strong back and strong arms than by using a washboard regularly.

People kept trying to find ways to make clothes washing easier, and a number of machines were developed for reducing the drudgery by hand-operated, mechanical means, using levers and cranks. However, those devices, ingenious as they were, had to give way to—you guessed it—electricity.

Today, all the housewife has to do is dump a load of soiled garments into an automatic washer, turn a dial, and go away.

Once considered the most menial and depressing of work, giving rise to the expression, "Blue Monday," clothes washing now is child's play.

The hand wringer.

The Hand Wringer

As common as the washboard was the hand wringer which had two rollers to squeeze the water from freshly washed clothing. The boy of the family often was pressed into service to turn the wringer on washday and had to be careful because a careless lad sometimes would get his fingers caught in the rollers. The wringer generally was mounted on the edge of a laundry tub.

The electric wringer attached to an electric washing machine was the first successor to the hand wringer, and now the automatic drier has eliminated the wringer from many homes.

Irons on stove.

The Flatiron

Those women who never have known anything but today's electric iron, with its heat selector, have missed a lot. Before electricity, ironing and pressing were done with a heavy, solid iron, shaped much like the electric iron of today, which was heated on top of a stove until it reached the desired temperature. Its readiness for use was judged either by gently spitting on the bottom or gingerly tapping a finger on the heated surface.

To avoid loss of time, the presser kept several irons on the stove so that one always would be hot, thus giving rise to the expression, "Having several irons in the fire."

At first, the handle was attached to the iron and became as hot as the iron itself; so it had to be wrapped with things resembling pot holders while in use. Later the detachable wooden handle was invented, which could be removed while the iron was being reheated.

A variation of the old flatiron was the charcoal iron, which contained a compartment into which live charcoal was placed. This type was handy when there was no stove or when the pressing was to be done at a distance from the stove.

A coffee mill.

The Coffee Mill

Until not so long ago, every home had a coffee mill so that the family could buy its coffee in the bean and grind it fresh for every meal. Some homes still have one, but most of us got rid of the mill and now let the manufacturer do the grinding. The coffee may not be quite as fresh but it's a lot less work.

The Ice Cream Freezer

Ice cream used to taste even better than it does today, and for several reasons. First, it was made from the finest of ingredients—fresh cream, fresh fruit, and so on. Second, you didn't have it so often, so it always was a special treat. Third, if you were a young boy, you did most of the hard work in making it and were really hungry for it when the time came to have a big helping.

Ice cream freezer.

Ice cream in those days was made only in the home, in an ice cream freezer which consisted of a wooden tub containing a metal can equipped with a crank and a paddle that were turned by hand. The freezing was accomplished with the aid of crushed ice, rock salt, and plenty of muscle. One reward for turning the crank was the privilege of licking the paddle after the task was finally completed.

Of course, the variety of flavors was limited, nothing like the assortments the ice cream stores and refrigerated peddler trucks have today, but the narrow choice of vanilla, chocolate, fresh peach, and fresh strawberry was all anyone asked for in those days.

After disappearing completely, the ice cream freezer has reappeared on a limited scale like some other vanishing Americana, but the store-made product still gets the big play.

Baking bread.

Baking Bread

It used to be said that Sunday was go-to-meeting day, Monday was washday, Tuesday was ironing day, Wednesday was mending day, Thursday was get-together day, Friday was cleaning day, and Saturday was baking day; and Grandma followed that schedule religiously. Some housewives still adhere to some such routine, except that Saturday's baking has dwindled to practically nothing in most homes.

Before the day when you could go to the supermarket and buy loaves of bread already sliced, enriched with vitamins, and especially treated to delay staleness, baking a week's supply of bread was a regular chore on Saturday for every housewife or some other female in the household.

And Grandma didn't stop with bread and rolls. She also baked a pie or two and at least one cake and maybe some doughnuts. Licking the dish in which the frosting for the cake was made and the spoon that stirred it was a special reward for the well-behaved boy—who might have helped by stirring the frosting and the cake batter.

Homemade bread like Grandma used to bake has long been held up as one of the highest gastronomical treats but, somehow, almost everyone, including Grandma, has become well satisfied with store bread these days.

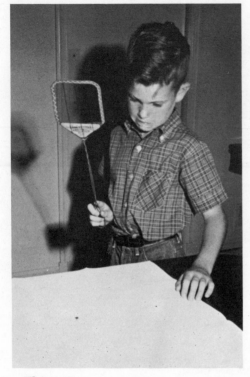

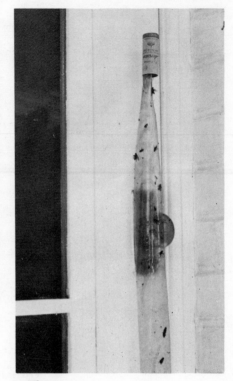

Fly swatter.   Fly paper.

The Fly Swatter

The common housefly (*Musca domestica*) had been a pest for many years when some genius invented the fly swatter and flypaper. The term "housefly" is, of course, a misnomer, since the two-winged insects are found also in barns, restaurants, barbershops, and many other places.

The fly swatter in its early stages of development consisted of a piece of pliable wire screening with bound edges, attached to the end of a stick.

Flypaper consisted of sheets of heavy paper coated with a flavored, sticky substance that attracted flies and then mired their feet so they could not escape. In another form, flypaper also appeared in a loose roll that could be suspended near a doorway to lure and snare flies as they started to fly inside.

The development of DDT and other insecticides has made the fly swatter and flypaper almost passé in most areas.

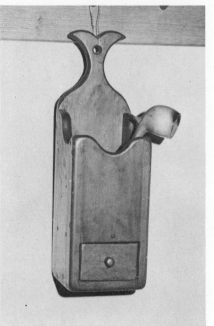

A match container.

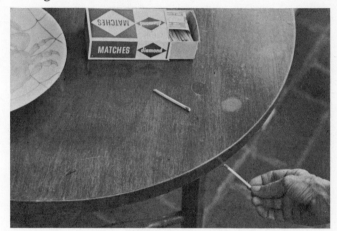

Long wooden match.

The Long Wooden Match

There was a time when the long wooden match, which lit when you scratched it on the seat of your pants or when you struck it against the underside of a table top, had the field all to itself. A supply of these matches would be kept in a wooden container hung on the kitchen wall or in a cardboard box near the gas stove—before the invention of the pilot light.

However, the wooden match often lit up without being struck, because of accidental friction or even the gnawing of a rodent. It has come to be replaced by the wooden box of safety matches, which are similar in shape to the long wooden matches, but smaller, and which light up only when scratched on the special material on the sides of its box, or on some similar material.

Following the safety match have come the space-saving book of paper matches, and finally the mechanical lighter.

The long wooden match is now used almost exclusively by pipe smokers, many of whom prefer it because it burns longer and is thus more likely to get the tobacco lit.

Wardrobe.

The clothes tree.

The Wardrobe

Resourceful and ingenious as our forefathers were, it took them a long time to think of the clothes closet. As a result, bedrooms in many of our finest old homes had no closets whatsoever. The ugly clothes tree was one substitute, but for those with an ample assortment of clothing, something more was needed—so the wardrobe was devised. It was nothing more than a free-standing closet, with one or two doors, that could be placed against a wall.

Many wardrobes were show pieces, made of choice hardwoods, handsomely carved and finished. Often the doors held full-length mirrors.

The built-in closet, which is less expensive and takes up less room, has replaced the wardrobe in newer homes, and closets have finally been built in corners of many older homes as well.

A place for everything—   —and everything in its place.

The Roll-Top Desk

Before there was such a thing as a private secretary or a visible index filing system, any man of substance, whether he was a businessman, professional man, or farmer, kept his papers and records together in his desk, and it was handy to have a separate compartment or pigeonhole for each type of paper: bills, receipts, letters to be answered, and so on.

This need led to the development of the roll-top desk which had several rows of pigeonholes, plus numerous drawers, and a flat surface on which to write. The advantage of the roll-top was that the owner of the desk could lock up everything by merely rolling down the top of the desk and turning a key. There was no need to hide anything or even straighten up the desk at the end of the day if the owner didn't wish to do so.

Another advantage of this system was that you never had to wonder where anything was. All you had to know was which pigeonhole to look in or which drawer to search through. Nowadays, of course, every businessman worthy of the name has one or more flat-top desks without a trace of a pigeonhole. There may be a few drawers for special documents but the rest of the papers are turned over to his secretary.

The ladies used to have neat little lap desks for their letter writing and, of course, all desks of whatever style were equipped with a quill pen.

Lap desk.   Quill pen.

Brass cuspidor.

The Cuspidor

Until not too many years ago, almost every home that harbored a user of tobacco had a cuspidor or spittoon that served as a receptacle for cigar butts, pipe dottle, and the like. The invention of the ashtray, the decline in per capita consumption of cigars and chewing tobacco, and the gradual assertion of authority by members of the feminine sex have brought about the virtual abolition of the cuspidor in the home. It now is found only in police stations, post offices, barbershops, and other public places.

Cuspidors often were round brass receptacles with flaring tops, set on rubber mats. Sometimes, though, especially in refined homes, they were flat, round china containers with removable lids, daintier than the brass model. No one seems to deplore their rapid disappearance.

The coal bin.

The Coal Bin

When the blessings of central heating first came to the American home, coal was the fuel universally used. This meant that each home gave over a part of its basement to a coal bin, a partitioned storing area near the furnace.

The coal went into the basement through a basement window or a special coal door. It was dumped in from bags or from a wheelbarrow or slid down a metal coal shute, which was carried by the horse-drawn coal wagon or cart delivering the fuel. There always was a certain unavoidable amount of coal dust in the air when a new delivery was received, and this dust made something of a mess in the basement, if not on the floor above.

Central heat register.

The wide coal shovel was found in every basement where there was a coal furnace, and the boy of the house spent a good part of his life shoveling coal into the furnace and removing ashes from the ashpit as it became full. The furnace often needed attention at the most inconvenient hours, such as early in the morning.

Removing the ashes was dirty work, and it was best to wear a hat or cap, because, if you didn't, the dust from the ashes made it almost impossible to get a comb through your hair. The ashes usually were removed in a metal basket and dumped in a bin out by the alley to be hauled away by the trash collector, or ashman, as he was called in those days. Today, of course, the coal bin has given way to the recreation room in most homes.

Before the electric fan was adapted to the hot-air heating system, the coal furnace was located near the center of the house to make it easier to pipe hot air to all rooms, although in some homes there was just one large heat register near the middle of the first floor.

Former carriage house.

The Carriage House

Many town people had a carriage house for their horse and carriage or buggy, especially physicians who needed transportation to make calls on patients, and bankers and merchants who could afford such luxuries.

The carriage house usually was located in back of the house, on an alley, with maybe a porte-cochere and a driveway leading out to the street through a stone gateway. The former served as a protection from the elements when boarding or leaving the vehicle.

Some carriage houses were so well designed and so substantial that, if not located on alleys, they have been converted into residences or offices. Others are used as garages if they are wide and long enough for today's mammoth cars.

Carriage house as home.

Stone gateposts.

A porte-cochere.

Female Accessories

The personal devices used by the feminine sex are numerous and ever-changing. For example, women used to select their shoes with an eye to utility before the day of the paved street and the automobile, which have minimized the hazards of walking. Now that there is little danger of stepping into mudholes or deep puddles and little occasion to walk long distances when the temperature is low and the ground covered with snow, anything that keeps the dainty feminine foot from touching the ground or pavement is accepted as a shoe.

In the old days, however, feminine shoes were much more substantial. They covered the foot and ankle completely and often included a good part of the leg, or limb as it was then known. The high-button shoe is best remembered, perhaps, because it seems so wholly impractical today (milady wore high-lace shoes, too). The button shoe, whether high or low, required a buttonhook, which is just as hard to find today as a button shoe.

Before the day of bobbed hair, pageboy cuts, poodle cuts, and the like, when most women wore their hair waist-long or longer, a hair receiver was seen on every dressing table. Milady put in the receiver any hair that came loose while combing.

The hair receiver was a small round glass or china receptacle with a lid that had a hole in the center through which the loose hair could be inserted. It served both to dispose of the loose hairs and to collect them in case madame wanted to make a rat for putting her hair in a bun or in other arrangements.

Drinking from a glass or cup always was quite a problem for a lady confined to bed. She either had to lean forward and raise up in a very awkward manner or else drink while lying flat and risk letting some of the liquid run down her neck. This was uncomfortable whether the liquid was hot or cold.

One solution was the invalid cup which had a long spout that curved downward, something like the spout on an oil can. In recent years, the introduction of the bent glass straw, as used in hospitals and sick rooms, has made the invalid cup obsolete.

Feminine eyeglasses have undergone drastic change in a relatively few years. Disappearing rapidly have been the glasses with small metal frames, those with metal temples and no frames, and the pince-nez which had no frames at all and no temples, but stayed in place because of a spring which gave them a tight grip on the bridge of the nose.

These early types of glasses have been replaced by harlequin glasses, which give the wearer an oriental look, and by glasses with heavy horn rims and temples. It is only fair to say that men also have worn all of the types mentioned, except the harlequins.

When the ladies used to wear long hair and big, floppy hats, the hatpin was standard equipment. Used principally to keep hats from blowing off in the wind, the hatpin also was very useful for warding off molesters and discouraging overly amorous males. The hatpins were kept in a special hatpin holder from which milady could select the right pin for the particular hat she intended to wear.

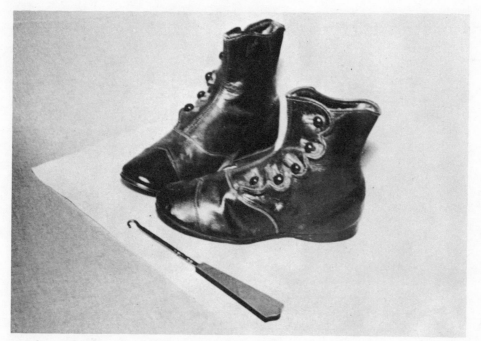

A buttonhook.

The hatpin.

The pince-nez.

High-lace shoes.

Hatpin holder.

A hair receiver.

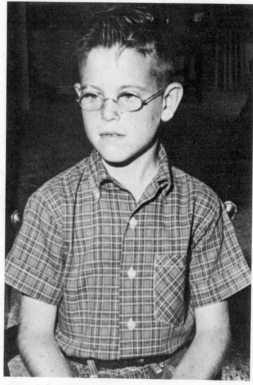

Metal-frame glasses.

High-button shoes.

The invalid cup.

Male Accessories

The life of a young male used to be quite a bit more complicated than it is today. For one thing he had to wear spats, which look like the upper part of a high shoe. The spats were worn on formal occasions with his patent leather dancing pumps and also when walking in the snow with low shoes.

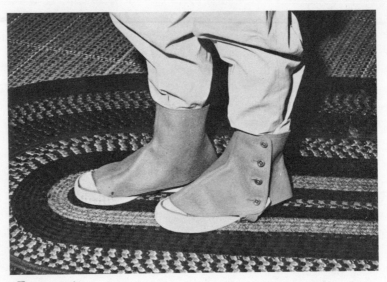

Fancy spats.

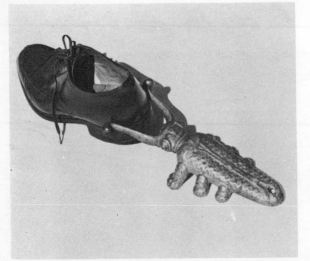

Before oxfords came into general use, heavy boots were worn by many men. To remove the boots, a bootjack was needed.

A bootjack.

An ivory-headed cane.

A pearl stickpin.

Hallmarks of the stylish man were the cane and the necktie stickpin. The stickpin, placed just below the knot, was both ornamental and functional. There often was a figure or a precious stone at the top of the pin, and the pin itself kept the two ends of the tie together. Today's tieclasp serves the same purposes.

A little snuff box, made of china or silver, used to be standard equipment in many drawingrooms and in some boudoirs, too, before cigars and cigarettes became popular. Made of powdered tobacco, snuff was utilized by placing a pinch on the back of one's hand and then sniffing it through a nostril where it imparted a sensation that presumably gave a peculiar satisfaction to the user.

The snuff box was used to hold the snuff after its wooden or cardboard container had been opened. Snuff was used by both men and women. It still is used to a limited extent by miners and factory workers who can't smoke on the job, but the ornate snuff box is found today only among the curios.

Snuff box.

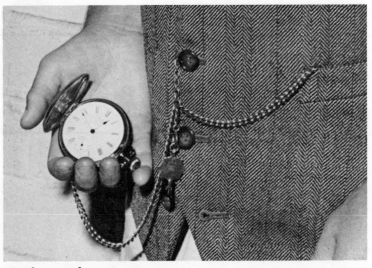

Pocket watch.

Every young boy looked forward eagerly to the day when he would receive his very own gold or silver pocket watch, which generally came to him as a high-school graduation present, or perhaps on his twenty-first birthday. The large timepiece, known sometimes as a turnip because of its size and thickness, was attached to a watch fob or the end of a watch chain that stretched across the owner's chest. In the former case, the watch was kept in a watch, or change, pocket just below the belt on the right-hand side of the trousers.

The watch chain was much preferred by those who had a Phi Beta Kappa key or some other fraternal insignia to display on it and also by those who had won gold footballs or basketballs in recognition of athletic prowess.

The wrist watch, regarded at first as the mark of a sissy, finally won out over the pocket watch by virtue of its greater convenience. So, pocket watches are a novelty today.

Male headgear also has changed. When the old iron derby, known also as a bowler and sometimes pronounced darby, finally went out of style, some predicted that it never would return—the reason being that it was both unbecoming to the men who wore it and also uncomfortable. The derby usually was black but also came in gray and brown.

It has not returned, although close variations have come onto the market for those very few men who think they look good in that type of hat.

119

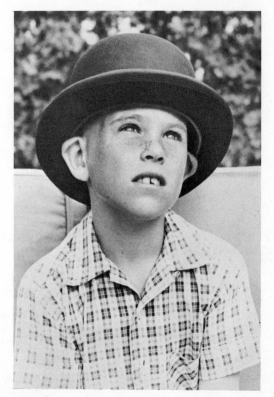

Derby.

The Male Toilette

In the days when a man used to wear his shirt two or three days between changings, a detachable collar was an absolute necessity, because collars became visibly soiled and had to be changed at least daily.

Shirts were worn longer between washings in those days, both because men were less fastidious and because the heavy underwear they wore absorbed some of the perspiration that makes it seem advisable to change shirts more often today.

Detachable collars, held in place by collar buttons, were first made of rubber and celluloid, which could be cleaned in a jiffy with soap and water. Then starched linen collars came into vogue in all shapes—from standup to turnover, up to two inches or more high, such as President Hoover used to wear, to the turndown collars that resembled the soft collar so popular today.

Standup collars still are worn with full-dress suits and cutaways, but few men own any other kind of stiff collar these days.

Detachable starched cuffs also were used by men who wore detachable collars, so that clean cuffs could be had without changing shirts every time the cuffs became soiled.

Waterproof collars.

One hazard that the adolescent male of today and tomorrow need never face in his own home is the straight-edge razor. Before the safety razor came on the market, the straight-edge was the only razor available. If it was sharp enough to give a clean and comfortable shave, it also was sharp enough to make numerous cuts in the tender skin of anyone not skilled and confident in its use. Many a lip and cheek and chin were gashed or scraped by straight-edge razors in the hands of inexperienced youths.

Being venturesome as they are, young boys seldom hesitated to try out Dad's straight-edge when they felt the time had come for their first shave. However, many a boy waited quite a spell before the second try because of the facial damage that so often occurred, and because Dad usually was quite upset to find that someone had dulled his prize razor.

Some men never did come to trust the straight-edge in their own hands and made a practice of going to the barbershop for a professional shave.

Except in barbershops, the safety razor and more recently the electric razor have completely replaced the straight-edge and the razor strop on which it was sharpened, just as the tube of shaving cream and the squeeze bottle have largely replaced the shaving brush and mug that once graced every bathroom where there was a male of shaving age.

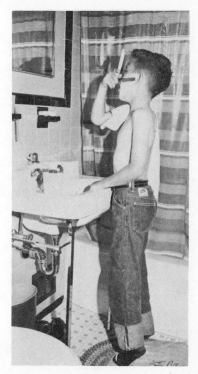

Straight-edge razor.

A shaving mug.

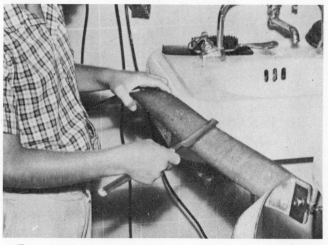

Razor strop.

121

A must for the males with mustaches was the mustache cup, which had a built-in shelf to keep coffee or other liquid from wetting the bushy mustaches, so common in the old days. The shorter mustaches worn today don't require special crockery.

Men's haircuts also have undergone a drastic change. At one time, those men who still had any hair wore it long because a "good head of hair" signified manhood, and was attractive to women. You heard such expressions as, "She ran her fingers through his hair," indicating both admiration and affection. If the long, thick hair was curly, so much the better.

Before the day of padded headguards, football players had to wear their hair long to avoid cranial injury. Other less athletic males found it advisable to follow the lead of the football heroes, even if they were not currently interested in a female.

All that has changed, however, and girls now can't run their fingers through a man's hair because it is much too short. Even if he doesn't wear a crew cut or flattop or butch cut, the younger man, and some older ones, too, wear their hair short.

A mustache cup.

3. Our Changing Towns

That our towns and cities have been undergoing a radical change isn't news, but some of the fundamental changes that are taking place have received little recognition. Everyone can see that store fronts are being modernized, older buildings are being rehabilitated and air-conditioned, new buildings and parking lots are replacing old structures, big buildings are replacing little ones, and big businesses are taking over the functions of lesser ones. But that is only part of the story.

Some businesses which once were as basic to everyday life as air and water have disappeared entirely or else have been absorbed by larger ones. Enterprises which were considered as essential as City Hall are gone forever. One single development, the displacement of the horse and wagon by motor vehicles, has brought about sweeping changes in what the eye sees as it looks upon the downtown area.

Contrary to the trend of our farms where specialization is the rule, the trend on Main Street is to combine specialties into one large operation as has happened in the department store and the supermarket.

Downtown itself has not begun to vanish but in many places, both large and small, it has stopped growing and may even be shrinking because of the radical changes that are occurring, including the mushrooming of suburban shopping centers.

Just as many people have not been aware that the haystack and the corn shock are virtually extinct, many of them have not noticed certain equally fundamental changes in town life, such as those pictured and described here.

Cobblestone street.

The Cobblestone Street

In horse and wagon days, when speeds were low, the cobblestone street was entirely satisfactory. It was noisy and unpleasant to ride on, but it was inexpensive and a lot better than a dirt road.

But the cobblestone surface disappeared fast as automobiles and trucks began to multiply, not only because the tires slipped on the stones, but also because vehicles and passengers would be shaken to pieces if driving speeds exceeded five miles an hour.

Since brick proved little better than cobblestones, asphalt and concrete are used on most of our roads. Cobblestones either have been taken up or else covered over, except on streets where traffic is negligible or the stones are regarded as good local atmosphere.

124

A small, empty trough.

The Horse Trough

One facility found in the smallest village as well as the largest city was the horse trough, where the hard-working draft and carriage horses quenched their thirst after making the long trip to town or hauling a heavy load from the depot.

Downtown could no more have been without one or more horse troughs in the olden days than it could get along without traffic lights today, but the trough has gone with the horse. And when you finally discover one in an out-of-the-way place, where the overly efficient road builders have not come upon it, the chances are that it is bone dry for lack of patronage.

These once indispensable troughs were made of stone, brick, cast iron, or concrete, not to mention wood, and were filled either by hand pump or public water supply. If the horses were really hot and dry, the driver let them have only a little water at a time, lest they become ill. Sometimes on a hot day, you saw a long line of thirsty horses waiting for a turn at the trough.

Horse drinking.

The Hitching Post

Where the parking meters stand today on downtown streets, you once saw a row of hitching posts, which served to park the horse as we park our autos today. No one, though, thought to charge for the privilege of tieing a horse at the curb.

Hitching posts took several forms, most typically a post with a ring at the top through which to tie or hook the hitching strap. The posts were made of wood, metal, stone, brick, or concrete. Some had figures, such as horses' heads, at the top for ornamental purposes. The bottom end was sunk solidly in the ground and held firm if the horse became frightened or unruly.

In addition, there were the hitching ring attached to an anchor buried in concrete and the hitching rail, a horizontal pole supported by two end posts, to which several horses might be hitched.

When no hitching device was available, the driver fastened the hitching strap to a heavy metal weight, carried for just that purpose, which was lowered to the ground. A horse might be able to walk away with a hitching weight, but he couldn't very well run—so it was better than nothing.

Gone with the hitching post that stood in front of every home, as well as every store, is the carriage block, a stone or concrete step placed at the curb to make it easier to enter or alight from a vehicle.

Hitching post.

A carriage block.

A hitching rail.

Horse weights.

The old and the new.

Once a livery stable.

The Livery Stable

The predecessor of the garage and the parking lot was the livery stable, located downtown, usually near the hotel, where travelers could leave their horses overnight. It was also the place where a horse and buggy or a saddle horse could be rented by the day or hour.

When the traveler drove his horse up to the hotel to stop for the night, a groom would take it to the livery stable where it would be watered, fed, rested, and groomed, ready to resume the journey the next day, just as our automobiles are stored and cared for overnight in a garage.

A handful of old livery stables remain today but few are used for stabling horses. In many communities it is difficult to determine where the old livery stable was located, if indeed the person you question knows what in the world you're talking about. A faint, old, painted sign, such as appears above and to the left of the door in the photograph, often is the only clue.

Being the scene of considerable activity, the livery stable was a social center for the temporarily unemployed and others who had time on their hands, despite the fact that, except to the dedicated few, it was a malodorous place.

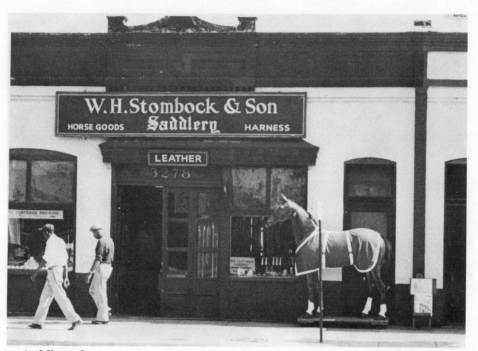

Saddlery shop.

The Harness Shop

Horses needed harnesses, so in the old days the harness shop was another important place of business in every town of any size. If the community was too small to support a shop making and dealing only in harness, the more essential items could be purchased from the general store or perhaps a feed store.

Harness shops also carried saddles and other articles used by and in connection with horses, such as feed bags and whips. This type of trade is carried on today in places known as saddlery shops, many of which are the same old harness shops trading under a more modern name.

129

A feed bag.

The sidesaddle.

The Sidesaddle

When ladies first began to ride horseback in public, they wore a divided skirt and used a sidesaddle which enabled the rider to sit with one knee around the pommel and both feet on the same side of the horse. Livery stables and harness shops both had to keep this item on hand.

Inasmuch as the arrangement was awkward, regardless of its advantages, the gentler sex gradually abandoned the sidesaddle in favor of the English and western saddles used by male riders. They then were able to ride faster and harder and could keep up better with the men in jumping their mounts. Moreover, they gained a more secure perch on the mount.

Wagon works sign.

The Wagon Works

Also gone from the present-day scene are the wagon and carriage works which once flourished in many communities. The function of those establishments was to make and repair wheeled vehicles for both farmers and cityfolk.

Such farm wagons as are produced today are turned out by farm implement manufacturers and run on rubber-tired, steel wheels, instead of the old wooden wheels of yesteryear.

In the days when there was an active demand for a half dozen or more types of carriages, carriage-making was a bustling local enterprise which since has been absorbed by a handful of auto manufacturers.

A sled.

The Delivery Wagon

At one time, deliveries to the town home from local merchants were made by horse and wagon, except when the goods were transported by bicycle or on foot.

Thus, homes were visited more or less regularly by the grocery wagon, butcher wagon, milk wagon, bakery wagon, ice wagon, coal wagon, peddler wagon, junk wagon, and sometimes a fish wagon. Traffic congestion was not uncommon in residential neighborhoods in those days.

When heavy snowfalls came, many of the merchants switched to horse-drawn sleds to make their deliveries.

Bakery wagon.

A junk wagon.

132

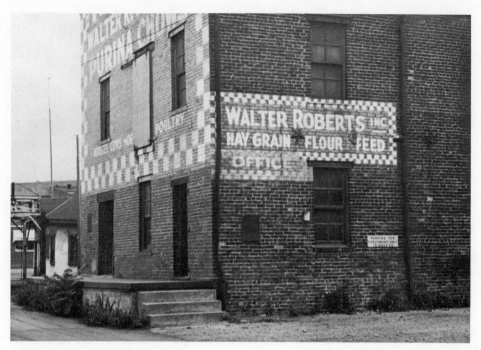

Hay, grain and feed store.

The Hay, Grain, and Feed Store

You still can find feed stores in any community, but when you get there the chances are you'll see nothing but bird and dog food. Hay and livestock and poultry feed just aren't enough in demand these days to support in-town stores having so limited a line. If available anywhere in town, those items can be obtained from hardware and farm implement stores, which also handle straw and seeds.

Here is another case where a type of business that once had a distinct identity and a large clientele has had its diminishing demand absorbed by establishments performing a wider service and carrying a more varied line of products.

The butcher's balance scales.

The Butcher Shop

Every town, big or little, had a butcher shop, also known as a meat market, where the butcher and his helper sold meat and meat products only. He handled sausage and scrapple which he made himself, and tripe and chitterlings, as well as beef, pork, veal, and lamb. Often he also sold chickens and turkeys and perhaps fresh and salted fish. Today, you have to hunt pretty hard to find such a shop, with its butcher block and the sawdust on the floor to absorb anything that fell.

Even if the sign outside says, "Meat Market," you find when you enter that the butcher has had to convert to a food store handling groceries, produce, and a line of frozen foods as well as meat. The modern housewife wants to buy everything under one roof.

Moreover, the butcher as we knew him once is disappearing rapidly. Instead of the husky, friendly, talkative man who deftly wielded his sharp knife and saw and cleaver on the block behind the counter, cutting steaks, chops, and roasts to order, we now have a meat cutter, an anonymous individual, who cuts up carcasses to be packaged and placed in a display counter, complete with price tag. To confer with a butcher or meat cutter in a supermarket, you ring a bell and presently he appears to answer your question and/or complaints.

Perhaps the old-fashioned butcher did weigh his thumb along with the fillet, when the outmoded balance scale was in vogue, and maybe he was inclined to be a bit fresh, but at least he was flesh and blood, and you could tell him what you wanted and tell him your troubles, too.

Sawdust on the floor.

134

Fruit store.

The Fruit Stand

The retail fruit store and the downtown fruit stand used to be just as much a separate business establishment as the meat market, but in all but a few places the fruit dealer has lost his identity and become a department of the supermarket.

Contributing to the disappearance of the separate fruit store are the host of stands that have sprung up along our highways outside the city limits, many of which buy most of their stock in town, and also the array of frozen fruits that can be stocked by any merchant possessing the necessary refrigerated display case.

Shining up the apples to attract the eye of the passer-by and reworking the strawberries to keep the top layers looking firm and ripe are becoming lost arts as more and more of our fruit is sold by impersonal assembly-line methods.

Notions store.

The Notions Store

When Mother sat down to her sewing or mending and found she needed a package of pins or some elastic, she'd send little Jenny around the corner to the notions store which handled sewing supplies, plus a line of dry goods, hosiery, and the like.

Today, Mother does precious little sewing because she can buy high-quality, ready-made garments at such reasonable prices, and the supplies she needs for mending come from the variety or department store.

If Mother deplores the passing of the notions store which was so handy, she has herself to blame, at least in part, for if she had kept on making the clothes for the family it might still be there. As it is, the demand isn't enough to support a store that deals only in the traditional notions line.

The five and dime.

The Dime Store

Gone also in fact, if not in name, is the good old Five & Ten Cent Store, familiarly known as the dime store, which at one time sold nothing priced above ten cents. It was the place to buy school supplies, inexpensive toys like tops and jacks, candy, Halloween goods, and a host of other low-priced items.

Today, the dime store is known as a variety store and is well named. Some modern dime stores sell items priced up to $200—layettes for $15.95, men's suits for $22.75, air conditioners for $199.50—along with a handful of items priced at 5¢ or 10¢ and many more than can be had for 39¢, 89¢, or $1.79.

Some of these dime stores have kept the old five & ten cent store name, despite the greatly expanded price range. Others have dropped the subterfuge entirely.

They have taken over much of the notions and dry goods business, a large share of the candy trade, most of the school supply business, and also handle books, phonograph records, men's and women's underwear, lawn mowers, velocipedes, and a wide range of other merchandise.

The general store.

The General Store

Our smaller towns couldn't support separate grocery, meat, fruit, hardware, and notions stores, so they had their general stores, known also as country stores. They handled food, housewares, hardware, farm supplies, almost anything you might think of. If the general store was out of the particular size or brand that you wanted, you either took a substitute, waited for a new shipment to come in, or got back in your buggy and drove to the next town to get what you wanted.

Some general stores remain, but no one is building new ones. The farmer, who used to spend an hour driving his team to the nearest general store for a galvanized pail or a block of salt, gets in his car today and reaches a shopping center in a fraction of the time.

The trouble is that the shopping center doesn't have any cracker barrel to sit around on inclement days and no checkerboard where one could while the hours away with a friend or with the owner. And the managers of the stores in the shopping center always are too busy to gossip about crops or about the antics of the farmer's daughter.

Shelf display.

A coffee grinder.

A cracker barrel.

Candy jars.

Cookie caddies.

The Bulk Goods

Before we had cellophane and other modern wrapping materials, many of the food items that we buy today in packaged form were stocked and displayed in bulk. The quantities requested by the customer were weighed out as ordered and wrapped in manila paper or put into bags.

Items which came in boxes, cartons, jars, sacks, tubs, or barrels included: candies and cookies, crackers and biscuits, coffee and tea, sugar and flour, pepper and salt, dried fruit and vegetables, butter and lard, macaroni and spaghetti, cocoanut, syrup, and vinegar.

Today, factory packaging not only speeds up service in the store but also keeps the merchandise cleaner and fresher, and the customer probably gets short-weighted less often.

Tailor shop.

The Tailor Shop

A local businessman who enjoyed real prestige as a genuine craftsman was the tailor, who had his little shop around the corner or down the street from the center of town. His function was making and remodeling clothes for gentlemen and ladies. He did the whole job, helping select the cloth and the pattern, taking and recording the measurements, cutting the cloth, putting the garment together for a fitting, and then finishing up the job in every detail.

To survive, the tailor had to branch out. First, he took on cleaning and pressing, then he added a line of ready-made clothes for customers who wanted something in a hurry or who didn't want to pay the price for custom-made garments. More often than not, his shop became a haberdashery, and he sold ties, shirts, underwear, hats, shoes, and the rest.

The tailor too often operates today in the back room of a haberdashery, coming out on call to take measurements for an occasional suit or, more frequently, for an alteration job. Although he remains with us in goodly numbers, the tailor shop is becoming scarcer and scarcer.

Iceman with tongs.

Old ice wagon.

Ice card in window.

The Ice Wagon

One of the most frequently seen vehicles on the street in the summertime used to be the ice wagon. Pulled by one or more horses, it delivered blocks of ice to stores and homes. The ice wagon was usually driven by a husky individual, who also had to cut and weigh the ice and carry it, by means of ice tongs, to the icebox. To keep from freezing his shoulder and getting himself wringing wet, the iceman placed a leather blanket over the shoulder on which he carried the ice.

On hot days swarms of young boys followed the ice wagon from house to house and eagerly grabbed the chips of ice which fell from the scales when the iceman weighed and split the large cakes of ice. Sucking these chips helped keep the youngsters cool on hot days, just as the larger cakes of ice made life more bearable when served in lemonade or used to make ice cream.

Town homes had ice delivered regularly. To simplify the process each home had a card with large numbers, visible from the street, telling the iceman how much ice was wanted on that particular day. By changing the position of the card, the housewife could ask for 25, 50, 75, or 100 pounds. If the card didn't appear in the usual window, the iceman just drove by, assuming that no ice was wanted.

In winter you might see the same driver and the same horses delivering coal.

The potbellied stove.

The Potbellied Stove

Before the day of oil burners, gas furnaces, and electric heaters, a device commonly used for heating a public room was a potbellied stove, so called because of its shape. Made of cast iron, it burned either coal or wood.

In the colder areas of the country, the potbellied stove was found in almost every depot, store, post office, and livery stable. It served as a popular gathering place where conversation flowed freely while frosted toes, fingers, and ears were being thawed out.

Eventually it was crowded out by various types of automatic heaters which do not require frequent attention and, for some reason, do not attract crowds the way the old potbellied stove once did.

Cigar store.

The Cigar Store and Its Indian

A cigar store Indian.

Back when cigar smoking was more prevalent and when chewing tobacco and snuff were more popular, every town of any size had a cigar store which specialized in stogies, perfectos, and the like. It might have been called a tobacco shop but cigars were the backbone of the trade.

Today in many cities, we have places called tobacconist shops that sell pipes, pipe tobacco, and various smokers' accessories in addition to cigars and cigarettes, but the cigar store as such is rapidly fading from the scene. Even the addition of candy bars, cigarettes, pipes, and magazines didn't save the cigar store as its sale of cigars fell off, and as the drugstore and later the supermarket began to stock tobacco products. The cigar stand once found in every hotel lobby has been renamed the newsstand in recognition of the shift in the nature of its trade.

All but gone, too, is the life-sized wooden cigar store Indian which used to grace the entrance to many a cigar store, reminding the public of the wares available inside. Those Indians that remain are mostly confined in museums.

144

An old-time barber pole.

The Barber Pole

Just as the cigar store had its Indian, the harness shop its stuffed horse, and the furrier his stuffed bear to stand outside the premises as a form of outdoor advertising, so did the barbershop have its red and white striped pole to remind the passers-by to get their hair cut, singed, shampooed, and soaked with tonic.

Mounted on the ground, these poles stood four or six feet high. Then, with the coming of electricity, the simple wooden poles were replaced by mechanical devices that turn endlessly.

One by one, the large barber poles have disappeared, to be replaced with window signs or smaller revolving poles mounted on the walls, near the door or at some other prominent place where all will see them.

145

The Old Store Signs

For the benefit of customers who couldn't read, many old-time merchants adopted symbols which they used as outside signs to identify the type of establishment.

In addition to the barber pole and cigar store Indian which, by comparison with other signs, were larger or more pretentious, there were the pig, representing a meat market; a horseshoe, indicating a blacksmith; a pipe for a tobacconist; a mortar and pestle for a druggist; and so it went. The horse was used both by the veterinarian and the harness shop, so some of the less literate customers presumably became confused, if not misled.

The meat market sign.

The tobacconist's sign.

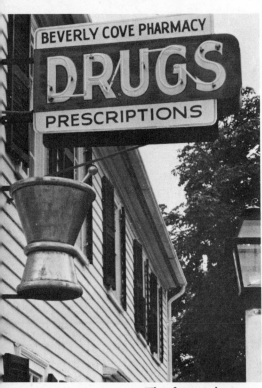

The druggist's sign.

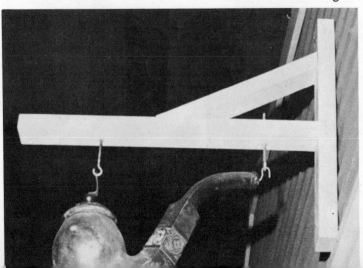

The veterinarian's sign.

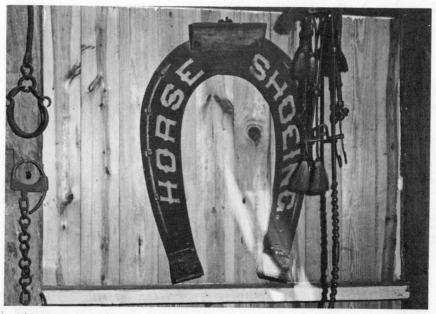

The horseshoer's sign.

Exterior of old shop.

The Blacksmith Shop

"Under the spreading chestnut tree
the village smithy stands. . . ."

The blacksmith used to be a mighty important member of any community. In addition to shoeing horses, he made and repaired tools, household equipment, farm implements, and other metallic objects. He pounded long and hard on his anvil and had to be a truly rugged man.

Blacksmith shops are hard to find these days because you can find in a store or mail-order catalogue most of the items the blacksmith used to make and because the electric welder has taken over the smith's function as a repairman. Thus his rhythmic workmanship, immortalized in the "Anvil Song," has been almost completely muted.

Interior of blacksmith shop.

Popcorn cart.

The Pushcart

Too few, indeed, are the neighborhoods which still see the old-time pushcart—with its little gas flames and shrill whistle—displaying its wares of peanuts, popcorn, and cracker jack. Others had for sale ice cream or fruit.

It's all too easy for the family today to hop into the car and drive to the nearest drugstore or snack bar when they feel the urge for refreshments. So, they don't have to wait for the uncertain arrival of the hand-propelled pushcart with its limited assortment. The pushcart, like the bullcart, has become uneconomic.

A peanut vendor.

The hurdy-gurdy.

The Hurdy-Gurdy

One of the real treats in the old days was to hear the organ grinder playing familiar tunes while his pet monkey, with the little red hat in hand, went about the crowd soliciting pennies at the end of his chain. The little fellow seemed almost human in the way he would reach for a coin or catch it in mid-air and then scurry to deposit the money in the tin cup held by his master.

Since we felt a bit guilty if we enjoyed the music and the monkey without contributing, Dad or Mother always was under pressure to let us have a penny or two to be handed to the little monkey in appreciation.

The organ grinder hibernated during the winter, so hearing the familiar tune again was a sure sign that spring was back, or at least on the way. The hurdy-gurdy, as the organ was familiarly known, would help greatly to brighten up present-day life.

Peddler wagon.

The Peddler Wagon

Occasionally you still see a peddler truck in some residential areas, bringing a load of fresh fruits and vegetables to the customer's door. The old peddler wagon, however, is all but gone.

Driving his one-horse wagon with its roof and built-in shelves, the peddler once was a familiar sight with his load of strawberries, raspberries, blueberries, peaches, plums, apricots, pears, sweet corn, squashes, tomatoes, celery, etc., depending on the season. He did a good business until his customers acquired automobiles which enable them to shop around at various supermarkets and take the pick of the best.

151

Old mill and wheel.

The Old Grain Mill

"Down by the old mill stream . . ."

The American Indians ground their grain by pounding it with rocks. Farmers did, too, in the early days but soon began to take it to one of the many small mills (powered by water, wind, or animals) which appeared in every community. Various methods and kinds of machinery were used, but in general the grain—corn, wheat, buckwheat, barley, etc.—was ground between large stones.

The millstones, the mill wheel, the pond, the stream, and the raceway now are part of the country's romantic past. The treadmill, with which large dogs provided the power to grind grain or churn butter, is now a real curiosity.

A few of the old mills have been preserved, and you can see a good many old millstones about the country, but today's farmer sells or sends his grain to an electrically powered mill which processes it into commercial grades.

Millstones.

Large millstones.

A treadmill.

A bandstand.

The Village Bandstand

"Strike up the band!"

Every Saturday night, and oftener in warm weather, we thrilled to the music of a local band playing in the wooden bandstand in the village square or in the park on the edge of town.

Sponsored by the high school, the firehouse, or some other civic group, the village band concert was a highlight of the week, eagerly awaited by all who loved good music, whether patriotic, popular, or semiclassical.

Radio, television, and the high-fidelity set have eclipsed the band concert in many towns, but its memories linger with all who used to enjoy the stirring weekly performances.

Roadside tavern.

The Roadside Tavern

A few of the lusty old roadside taverns that sprung up during stagecoach days still remain in business. They no longer try to attract overnight guests because the accommodations are rather primitive and remodeling might not pay. The number of taverns, not to be confused with beer parlors of the same name, is dwindling rapidly as new superhighways take over the right-of-way on which they are located or else divert traffic to new routes.

For the most part the roadside tavern has become a bar and restaurant, usually with a juke box to lure the younger trade, plus a coke machine so Dad and Mama won't hesitate to stop in when they have the youngsters along.

Roadside tavern.

155

Commercial hotels.

The Commercial Hotel

Until a short time ago the only place where traveling men, or drummers as they were called, and other out-of-town visitors could spend the night was in the small downtown commercial hotel. The typical hotel was located on Main Street or Broadway, near the principal intersection, and had a front porch with chairs where the guests could keep track of what was going on and who was going where. It also had a public dining room, often the only one in town worthy of the name, and a cigar counter and perhaps a bar.

If the old commercial hotel still stands, it probably has been converted into a boardinghouse with semipermanent guests who pay by the week or month. New kinds of competitors have taken the overnight customer.

Pool hall.

The Poolroom

The name, "Poolroom," may have all but vanished, but the establishment still is with us. Poolhalls or poolrooms now are generally known as billiard parlors—the original name having been dropped because it fell into disrepute.

The name of the game also has changed, from pool to pocket billiards. Billiards is thought of as a game played by gentlemen, whereas pool was frequently associated with unsavory characters, dubbed "poolhall bums" or "poolroom loafers." The latter, of course, tended to give the game and the places where it was played a bad reputation.

The modern billiard parlor usually has juke boxes, air-conditioning, and coin machines. It sells soft drinks along with whatever else it is licensed to serve.

Old-type saloon.

The ladies' entrance.

The Saloon

A few old-style saloons still remain, just about as they were before prohibition. But most have been replaced, often in name only, by the more socially acceptable cocktail lounge or tavern or the less stylish bar and grill.

Even where the saloon remains intact, its family entrance or ladies' dining room is now just another door. The patrons mix indiscriminately.

The bartender has changed very little, if at all, and in some establishments he has been replaced by a barmaid. The drink-on-the-house is heard of less often, and you seldom run into the free spender who used to stride into the bar, shouting "The drinks are on me. See what the boys in the back room will have!" The free lunch also is a thing of the past, although there may be free popcorn or peanuts.

A pillory.

The Whipping Post

Punishment for crimes and misdemeanors used to be more public and more humiliating than it is today. In addition to being confined in jail offenders were burnt at the stake, whipped, placed in stocks or a pillory, and submerged in water on a ducking stool.

The whipping was accomplished by tieing the wrists of the prisoner to rings at the top of a tall wooden post and then lashing the back, usually with a cat-o'-nine-tails.

A pillory consisted of wooden bars with openings in which the head, hands, and perhaps feet of the offender could be inserted, in a standing or sitting position. Ducking stools were seats at the end of long beams in which common scolds, cheats, thieves, drunks, and wife beaters could be confined while being ducked in a pond or pelted with debris.

159

The whipping post.

A man-drawn fire engine.

The Man-Drawn Fire Engine

The fire engine has gone through several stages of development. Prior to the red and chrome, gasoline-propelled monsters that respond to fire alarms today, there were the horse-drawn vehicles—the steam pumper, hose cart, and hook-and-ladder. Those horses really could step, too, spurred on by the loud and constant clanging of the gongs that served to alert the public and clear the streets.

And before that was the man-drawn pumper, pulled by husky volunteers who were selected for their fleetness of foot and soundness of wind. The runs were not long in those days, because towns were smaller. But time was a big factor when a fire broke out, and only the fastest runners were good enough for this important job.

A steam pumper.

Gas light.

Gas street lights.

The Gaslights

For some years the streets in our larger cities were lighted at night by illuminating gas, which gave off a yellowish, flickering light. The gas lamps were mounted atop tall cast-iron poles placed at the curb or at street intersections.

Gaslighting also was used for homes, both inside and out. The plugged-up ends of gas feed pipes can still be seen in the walls and ceilings of older homes and hotels, although in some places the electric wiring was led in through the pipes.

Hotels often found it necessary to post signs saying, "Don't blow out the lights," because the uninitiated extinguished the gaslight by blowing out the flame. This was wrong, since the gas kept coming and ultimately might asphyxiate the occupants of a closed room. The proper procedure was to turn off the gas by closing the valve which admitted it to the fixture.

Gas chandelier.

School desk.

School desk.

The Old School Desk

One kind of old school desk was a small oblong table with a slanting top that opened on hinges at the back for storage of books, pencils, and papers.

Another type was the small desk with a folding seat attached to its front for the pupil ahead. It had an inkwell into which a girl's long tresses might dip or get dipped, and there was space under the top for supplies.

The size of these desks varied according to the grade for which they were made, the lower grades naturally having the smaller sizes. These desks and seats were bolted to the floor, whereas today's desk seats are movable. Inkwells are completely out.

162

Vacant lot playground.

The Vacant Lot Playground

Any conveniently located vacant lot of sufficient size was utilized as an informal playground in the days before our local governments became flush with money and before there was so strong an awareness of the dangers of unregulated play.

It was on those lots that boys, and sometimes tomboys, played such versions of baseball as choose-up-sides, work-up, and one-o'-cat, together with such other games as touch football, pom-pom-pullaway, pig pile, hide-and-seek, run-sheep-run, and the like.

Vacant lots are becoming scarcer as new homes fill all available space. Moreover, the vacant lot playground is frowned on today because, in addition to annoying nearby residents, it lacks proper supervision. Special playgrounds with trained leaders are provided these days.

The calliope.

The animal wagon.

The Circus Parade

A standout feature when the three-ring circus came to town each year used to be the circus parade, which served to stimulate interest in the marvels to be seen under the "big top" on the edge of town.

The parade consisted of horse-drawn chariots and wagons containing lions, tigers, and other wild animals; plus elephants and their trainers; the sidesplitting clowns who performed their antics as they raced alongside the wagons; and then at the end of the parade the inevitable calliope, a horse-drawn organ that gave forth shrill but exciting music.

Calliopes also were found on the old paddlewheel excursion boats on inland rivers, serving both to entertain the passengers and entice additional customers aboard.

164

4. Our Changing Transportation

Methods of travel have changed even more quickly than most other aspects of American life, and the change continues unabated.

This becomes evident when we realize that large-scale travel by automobile is less than a half-century old and that mass travel by bus and airplane, which now are dominant in mass transportation, is less than a quarter-century old. Domestic travel by ferry, streetcar, interurban and elevated railroad, all of which were thriving and vital to the economy twenty-five years back, is shrinking fast.

Passenger traffic on the railroads is dwindling to the point where some major roads are begging for subsidies, and the future at best is uncertain. Only the subway and steamship travel to foreign shores seem to be holding their own among the older forms of public transportation.

Covered bridge.

The Covered Bridge

One of the more romantic remains of our past is the covered bridge, found mainly but not exclusively in the northeastern part of the country. Consisting of wooden sheds built over the bridge floors, they served to strengthen the bridges and prolonged their life by keeping the planks dry.

Although determined efforts are made by some tradition-conscious communities to preserve these picturesque structures, others seemingly care little about them. The result is that our covered bridges are disappearing one by one, victims of fire, flood, rot, and sheer neglect. And with each one goes part of our precious heritage.

Covered bridge.

Interior of bridge.

A prairie schooner.

The Covered Wagon

The prairie schooner or covered wagon or Conestoga wagon which played so prominent a part in the settlement of the Far West hasn't actually vanished because it is playing an equally prominent part in western movies and television programs.

Whether drawn by horses, mules, or oxen, the covered wagon made slow time by any standard. It nevertheless conveyed its owners and their possessions across the nation, at a time when there were no roads and many obstacles.

168

A stagecoach.

The Stagecoach

Like the covered wagon, the stagecoach has been kept fresh in our memories by television and motion picture so that it's just as familiar to the children of today as it was to the youngsters of the mid-1800's when it was a principal means of public transportation.

In addition to drivers and riflemen, marshals and sheriffs, desperadoes and dance-hall girls, the stagecoaches carried mail and freight, and ordinary citizens who had occasion to travel about the country.

By changing horses at regular intervals, these coaches were able to maintain a fairly fast pace but it's unlikely that they ever will make a come-back, except on the screen.

The Saddlebags

Standard equipment for the horseback rider in the old days was the saddlebags in which he carried personal belongings. Saddlebags usually were a pair of leather pouches fastened together with a strap or rope which was thrown across the horse's back, so that one bag hung on each side. Sometimes, though, there was only one bag which hung from the pommel of the saddle.

Saddlebags corresponded roughly to the glove compartment and trunk of today's automobile and came in various sizes.

Saddlebags.

Barging down the canal.

The Canal

The few canals in operation in this country are the remnants of the many that came into being in the early part of the nineteenth century, just before the advent of the railroad. Nothing could have been more badly timed.

Credited with having played a valuable part, temporarily, in opening up the eastern half of the country to settlement and development, the canal network at its peak measured something like 5,000 miles, counting mileage started but never completed. The Erie Canal in New York State and the Cap Cod Canal are the best known of all these artificial waterways.

Passengers and freight were hauled via barge, scow, and packet, the motive power coming from humans, horses, mules, and oxen. Humans powered the barges both with poles and by actually pulling them in simple harness on the same towpaths used by the animals.

Locks and gates were needed to cope with the differences in elevation along the canal routes. Tolls were collected at tollgates and tollhouses, and taverns sprang up in the vicinity of the locks to feed travelers and bed them down for the night. The custom of collecting tolls eventually went out of fashion, except on bridges and a few other places, until the modern turnpikes came along, charging roughly the same fees collected on the old canals.

Toll house.

Canal locks.

Canal tavern.

Ferry boat.

The Ferry

One by one, ferryboats are disappearing in the wake of newly constructed bridges and tunnels which accommodate much more traffic per hour at substantial savings in time to travelers. However, when time is not a factor, the ferry is missed by those motorists who used to enjoy the break in driving, with the chance to stretch their legs and perhaps consume refreshments while the ferry made its way to the opposite landing.

However, ferries are not missed very much by those drivers who used to experience long waits when traffic piled up at rush hours and on holidays.

Whether their power came from steam, diesel oil, or gasoline, the ferries moved at a relatively slow pace, introducing an element of leisure that is all too lacking in today's high-speed travel.

A whaling ship.

A figurehead.

The Sailing Ship

While sailboats are becoming more numerous than ever each year, the sailing ship is a museum piece—a few remain in service for training and other purposes. Before the appearance of the much faster steamship, the sailing vessels, with their tall masts, their vast area of sails, and their maze of ropes and pulleys, were used commercially and served as men-of-war into the nineteenth century.

Sailing ships also were used for other special purposes, such as hunting whales, transporting slaves, exploring far-off lands, colonizing, and pirating.

Most sailing ships had a wooden figure, known as a figurehead, mounted on their prow. Often intended to bring good luck, the figureheads sometimes were truly eye-catching and artistic. They served no purpose other than ornamental and gave rise to the expression denoting someone who contributes nothing but his name and presence to an undertaking.

173

A sidewheeler.

The Paddlewheel Steamer

In the days when passenger traffic was relatively heavy on our larger rivers, notably the Mississippi, Ohio, and Hudson, paddlewheel steamers were the principal means of water travel. The steamers were propelled by wooden wheels similar to those that turned a mill. The wheels were placed either on each side of the boat or at the back, or stern. They were turned by steam engines that burned wood or coal.

It was on these paddlewheelers, commemorated in song and poetry, that the Mississippi River gambler won his notoriety. A tall, suave rascal with sideburns, long coat, and tight pants, the gambler victimized all comers, country bumpkins as well as city slickers.

The paddlewheel steamers carried both freight and passengers and, before the day of the railroad, were the favored means of shipping cargo from east to west and north to south in the interior of the country.

The *Robert E. Lee.*

Early locomotive.

The Wood-Burning Locomotive

Wood, coal, electricity, gasoline, and diesel oil have been successively as fuel for the locomotives that have been operated on American railroads. In the early days when wood was the chief fuel, passengers were drafted to gather a new supply along the route when the fireman began to run short.

The coal-powered locomotive went through many stages of development before it reached its peak and attained monstrous proportions, especially the engines used to haul freight over steep and winding mountain grades.

Disappearing with the wood-burning and the steam locomotive is the distinctive and traditional steam whistle by which many people set their watches. The old *woooo-woooo-woo-woooo* of the steam engine has been replaced by the shriller whistle of the diesel locomotive which doesn't have the same emotional appeal to the listener.

Steam locomotive.

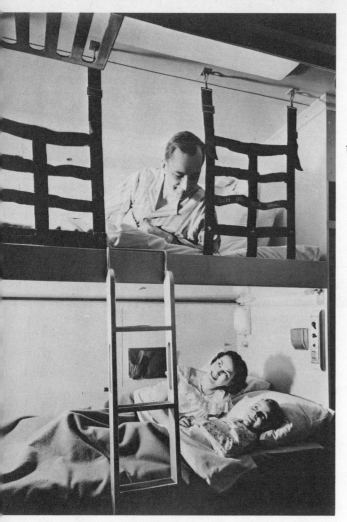

Upper and lower berth.

The Upper Berth

Hailed at first as ingenious, the upper berth has come to be recognized as an inconvenient way to spend a night on a train. The upper berth, which folded into the top of the sleeping car when not in use, was entered by means of a ladder. The ladder was removed by the sleeping-car porter when the passenger had ascended and was recalled by ringing a bell when the passenger was ready to descend from his lofty perch.

An upper berth cost quite a bit less than a lower berth, which was much easier to get into and out of. In a pinch, the upper could be used by two persons, preferably small ones.

A lower berth and the upper above it were called a section. Privacy was attained by heavy canvas curtains and a sliding panel which formed a brief partition between the sections.

The newly developed roomette and duplex roomette are cheaper than a bedroom, have private plumbing facilities, and offer much more privacy than either an upper or lower berth. They have gradually taken much of the demand, with the result that some railroads no longer quote rates on berths.

Old excursion poster.

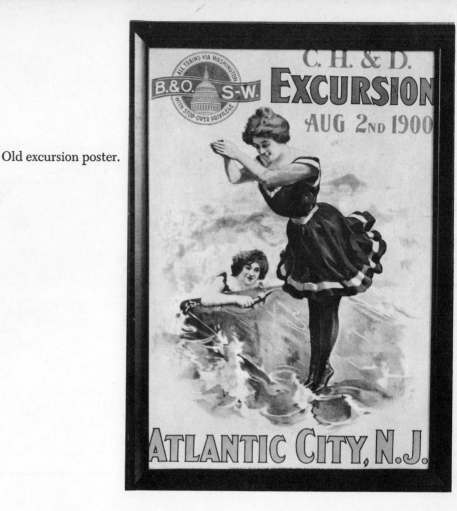

The Excursion Train

Before the day of the auto, opportunities for a change of scenery were relatively few, so the railroads used to organize special excursions to places of interest, such as the seashore or mountains or a nearby big city. The excursions usually were scheduled for a Sunday or holiday, and the equipment used consisted of coaches that ran in commuter service on weekdays.

These excursions usually started early in the morning and returned the same evening. The price of a round-trip ticket might or might not include some extra, such as a band concert or boat ride at the destination.

Rates generally were fairly low so that a workingman could take his wife, the kiddies, and maybe Grandpa or Aunt Meg for a reasonable outlay and have a whole day's respite from the routine of home. Mother usually packed a lunch.

Nowadays there is no need to wait for someone to organize an excursion. The family just gets in the car, leaving and returning when they wish, but running the risk of traffic jams and breakdowns that Dad wouldn't have to worry about on an excursion train.

We still hear of special excursions occasionally but they are known mostly as special trains. They go to such events as football games and to places like ski lifts, but the bulk of the people seem to prefer the auto.

An interurban.

The Interurban Electric Train

A onetime extensive network of electric interurban train service has shrunk to a small fraction of its former mileage. The speedy one-car and multiple-car trains, scooting at breakneck speed from one city to another with passengers and freight, now are seen in precious few localities as passengers have turned to buses, which have more flexible routes and more convenient terminals.

The traveling salesman used to depend on the interurbans extensively before the day of the company auto and the auto expense allowance.

Riding the fast-moving cars was one way to keep cool on hot summer days before air conditioning came along.

Old horse car.

The Streetcar

It seems like just a few years ago that the streetcar line was being hailed as a great asset to a growing town. It represented progress de luxe and definitely put the community above the small-town level.

First came the horsecar, then the electric car which got its current from overhead wires or from beneath the pavement. There were open cars for warm weather use, with canvas curtains in case of rain, and closed cars with windows that could be opened by any strong man.

The motorman operated the car in the front with the aid of a clanging footbell, while the conductor collected fares from his position in the rear, helped customers on and off, and called out the stops. Each fare was recorded on a register that rang a bell to show that the fare had been collected and counted the number of paying passengers. The early streetcar had plush or wicker seats, later made of leather or composition, and a huge searchlight which had to be moved to the other end of the car when it reversed directions at the end of the line.

The conductor eventually disappeared when efficiency experts demonstrated that the motorman could collect the fares, in addition to operating the car.

179

Old street car.

The streetcar was stopped by winding a brass crank in the early days, and the speed was regulated by turning a hand-operated lever. When a slow-moving horse and wagon got on the track ahead of a fleet car, the motorman indignantly clanged his loud bell—clang, clang, clang, clang—until the driver pulled off to the side.

Each car also had a cowcatcher, a sort of scoop, in front to catch any humans, animals, or other objects that might fall on the track before an oncoming car. Later this device was pointed like a snow plow, to push foreign objects to one side instead of scooping them up.

Economy of operation, flexibility of route, and greater average speed have given the bus an advantage which has led to the rapid disappearance of the streetcar, its tracks, and overhead wires.

The old carbarn which housed the streetcars usually is converted into a garage for the buses which replace them or else becomes a warehouse or small factory.

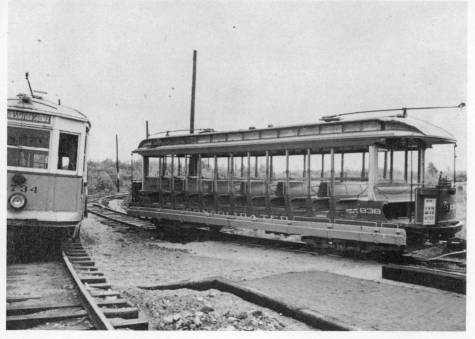

Old open car.

A cowcatcher.

Car barn.

Old highway marker.

The Highway Marker

Motoring across the country used to be a much less frantic matter than it is today—there were fewer cars and trucks and fewer through highways. Well known among the early trails were the Lincoln Highway, now U.S. 30; the National Road, now U.S. 40; and the Dixie Highway, now U.S. 1.

With fewer highways there was less chance of making a wrong turn, so it wasn't necessary to have as many highway markers as we have today. Nor were the markers as prominent as those found today on our turnpikes and highways.

Deemed sufficient identification in those days were occasional stone or concrete markers bearing the name or symbol of the highway, plus maybe a directional arrow and sometimes the mileage to the next big city.

Goggles.

Cranking a Model T.

The Linen Duster

Prior to World War I, one didn't start on a motor tour without a linen duster to cope with the dust encountered on virtually any road outside town. This special equipment, worn by both men and women, also was donned on days when recent rains had laid the dust, because it served as a sort of uniform for the privileged few. The ownership of an automobile was, for quite a few years, a mark of considerable social distinction.

Companion equipment for the owners of early autos included the veil for the lady, goggles for everyone, lap robe, ear muffs, leather gauntlets, and foot warmers. All of these were needed in the days when the roadsters and touring cars then in vogue were completely open, and side curtains afforded only partial protection from rain and cold.

These early cars had hand cranks instead of self-starters, and cranking was quite an art, especially on sub-freezing days.

The linen duster.

Veil.

Hand pump.

The Tire Repair Kit

In the days when four punctures per hundred miles were not uncommon on a cross-country "tour," every automobile was equipped with a hand pump, a jack, and a tire repair kit.

Today neither a pump nor a repair kit is found in the cars we drive. In the first place, the tires are so difficult to get on and off the rims that we couldn't possibly repair them without special equipment, and tire trouble is so infrequent that we can afford to call for professional help when it does occur.

Large-wheeled bike.

The Big-Wheeled Bike

Only in relatively recent years have the two wheels of a bicycle been the same size. In the olden days, the front wheel was larger, often much larger, than the rear one and the "wheel," as a bicycle sometimes was called then, was much more difficult to ride than the present-day type.

Another large-wheeled bike.

Acknowledgements

Invaluable assistance was received from many individuals and organizations in the preparation of this book. A number of the photographs were taken in private homes, antique shops, and museums, thanks to the fine people who were willing to share their treasures with others.

The author is deeply indebted to the following for the generous help they provided:

Mr. and Mrs. Jack P. Barker, Camp Inverness, Rockville, Md.
Dr. and Mrs. Steven O. Beebe, Sandy Spring, Md.
Mrs. William Dinwoodie, Sandy Spring, Md.
Mr. and Mrs. William J. Dorvillier, San Juan, P.R.
Mr. and Mrs. Merton A. English, Chevy Chase, Md.
Mr. A. Douglas Farquhar, Sandy Spring, Md.
Mrs. Emilie Fernsler, Washington, D.C.
Mr. Josiah Ferris, Mason's Neck, Va.
Mrs. William H. Gilpin, Olney, Md.
Mr. C. W. Hinden, Lancaster, Pa.
Dr. and Mrs. Joel B. Hoberman, Bethesda, Md.
Mrs. Josiah Waters Jones, Olney, Md.
Mr. Otis B. Kent, Rockville, Md.
Mr. Mahlon Kirk IV, Sandy Spring, Md.
Mrs. Charles C. Koones, Rehoboth Beach, Del.
Mrs. William H. Kricker, Sandy Spring, Md.
Mrs. John C. Larson, Bethesda, Md.
Mr. Thornton W. Owen, Rehoboth Beach, Del.
Mr. and Mrs. Arthur L. Quinn, Washington, D.C.
Mr. and Mrs. William M. Requa, Sumner, Md.
Mr. A. H. Smith Jr., Upper Marlboro, Md.
Mr. Dudley Smith, Mitchellville, Md.
Dr. and Mrs. Charles V. Stiefel, Washington, D.C.
Mrs. Frederic L. Thomas, Ashton, Md.
Mr. and Mrs. Harry W. Townshend, Mitchellville, Md.
Mrs. Robert Warner, Bethesda, Md.
Mrs. Millard F. West, Sr., Chevy Chase, Md.
Mr. and Mrs. J. Albert Willson, Brighton, Md.
The American Ice Company, Baltimore, Md.

The Amish Farm and Home, Lancaster, Pa.
The Association of American Railroads, Washington, D.C.
The Atheneum, Plymouth, Mass.
The Auto Museum, Salem, Mass.
Baltimore and Ohio Railroad, Baltimore, Md.
The Country Museum, Wickford, R.I.
D.C. Transit System, Inc., Washington, D.C.
The District of Columbia Fire Department, Washington, D.C.
Fontana Village, N.C.
Fort Mt. Hope, Ticonderoga, N.Y.
Fort William Henry, Lake George, N.Y.
Gaslight Club, Inc., Washington, D.C.
Gaslight Village, Lake George, N.Y.
Great Northern Railway
Hechinger Co., Washington, D.C.
Library of Congress, Washington, D.C.
Metropolitan Police Department, Washington, D.C.
Mystic Seaport, Mystic, Conn.
The New England Electric Society, Kennebunkport, Me.
Norfolk and Western Railway
The Peabody Museum, Salem, Mass.
The Pennsylvania Farm Museum, Landis Valley, Pa.
Pennsylvania Railroad, Philadelphia, Pa.
The Smithsonian Institution, Washington, D.C.
Sturbridge Village, Burlington, Vt.
The Vermont Country Store, Weston, Vt.
The Volta Bureau for the Deaf, Washington, D.C.

DATE DUE